The View From Down Here

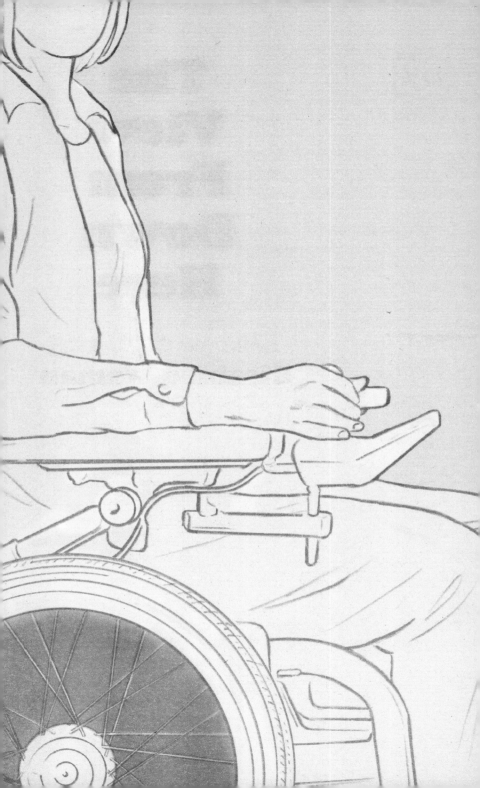

The View From Down Here

Life as a young disabled woman

Lucy Webster

Acquisitions Editor Marleigh Price
Project Editor Izzy Holton
Senior Production Editor Tony Phipps
Senior Production Controller Samantha Cross
Art Director Maxine Pedliham
Publishing Director Katie Cowan

Jacket Designer Mylène Mozas-Sauvignon
Jacket illustration by Sun Bai
Cover photograph by Ania Flaszczyńska

First published in Great Britain in 2023 by
Dorling Kindersley Limited
DK, One Embassy Gardens, 8 Viaduct Gardens,
London, SW11 7BW

The authorised representative in the EEA is
Dorling Kindersley Verlag GmbH. Arnulfstr. 124,
80636 Munich, Germany

A CIP catalogue record for this book
is available from the British Library.
ISBN: 978-0-2416-1276-7
Printed and bound in the United Kingdom

www.dk.com

MIX
Paper | Supporting
responsible forestry
FSC™ C018179

This book was made with Forest
Stewardship Council™ certified
paper - one small step in DK's
commitment to a sustainable future.
**For more information go to
www.dk.com/our-green-pledge**

**To all the disabled women who
came before and lit the way –
thank you**

Contents

chapter 1
Existing in the world 9

chapter 2
**My body: Acceptance
amid exclusion 30**

chapter 3
**Care: The radical case
for interdependence 60**

chapter 4
**Making friends: What does
it mean to fit in? 88**

chapter 5
**Creating community:
Finding my place 108**

chapter 6
**Dating:
Locked out of love 126**

chapter 7
**Motherhood:
Looking for hope 152**

chapter 8
**Towards a future
where everyone belongs 180**

Acknowledgements 204

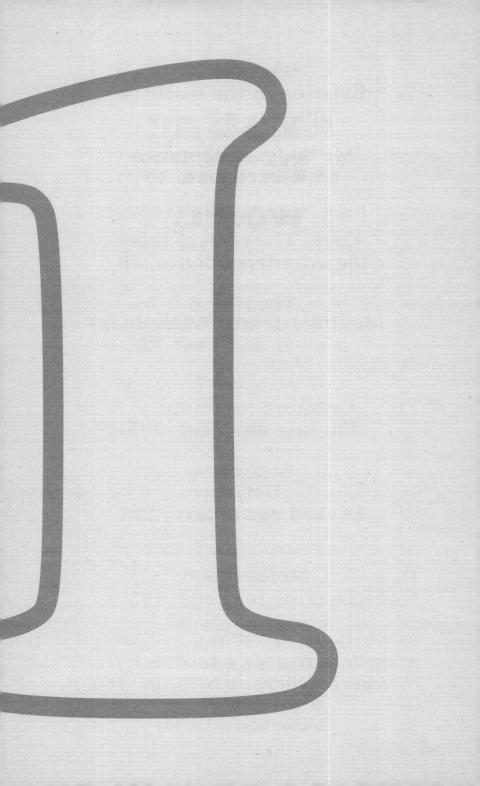

Chapter 1
Existing in the world

Let me tell you about the time a bouncer wouldn't let me into a club because I use a wheelchair. No, really.

Let's start with some context. It was a Saturday night, and my friends and I had headed out to Clapham to drink cocktails. We'd checked online that the bar was accessible – it even had a disabled loo. Success. We'd had a couple of drinks and were having a good time, but the bar was closing and we didn't want to head home. We wanted to dance. So, against my better judgement, I started googling accessible clubs in South London and, what do you know, there was one just up the road. *Bingo*, I thought.

For once it wasn't raining, and as we meandered down Clapham High Street we could see a short queue of people shuffling into the club. As ever, the rope line separating the queue from the rest of the pavement was too close to the wall for my wheelchair to fit through, so I took the opportunity to enjoy one of the few perks of disabled life and headed straight to the door. And then the trouble started.

'We can't let you in in your chair,' a bouncer said, as if this was the most casual statement in the world.

In that first split second, I thought he was telling me that my information was wrong – after all, most clubs in London aren't accessible, and online access information is extremely unreliable, so it wouldn't have been a surprise if the promised lift turned out to be mythical. Still, 'we can't let you in' was an odd turn of phrase, so I asked him to explain what he meant.

It transpired that the lift did indeed exist, and it was working. But the club was busy, he said, and he just wanted to 'keep me safe'. I was momentarily a little taken aback. I'd been refused entry to clubs before, but always because they'd assumed my access needs. Such open and blatant discrimination was rare.

'I'm used to busy, I'm from London,' I told him, my voice becoming strained as I tried to project authority over the din of the crowd and the traffic. Anyway, I could keep myself safe – I didn't need him to do it for me. He shrugged.

At this point, to make matters worse, another bouncer joined the increasingly surreal conversation. The second bouncer changed tack, switching from the claim that it was 'too busy' to one I genuinely wasn't prepared for: apparently the music was 'too rowdy' for me, and I wouldn't like it. It took me a while to process what I'd just heard.

'Are you seriously telling me the music is unsuitable for me?' I asked.

By now, I could feel my heart starting to pound, and I was trying harder and harder to keep my voice steady; to pretend I was not upset and angry. Any show of emotion would only have played into these two strangers' view of me as a vulnerable woman in need of protection.

The first bouncer quickly got bored of our back-and-forth and wandered off to simpler duties. Bouncer number two continued to look at me with a peculiar mix of contempt and pity. My friends tried, valiantly, to use reason and logic and a good deal of indignation, but I could see that the bouncer on the door didn't care. She was barely listening.

'Let's go,' I said, realising that I was no longer in the mood to entertain this woman's prejudices, let alone hand over money to a company with such blatantly discriminatory staff. She hardly noticed us walk away.

I tell this story because it is so perfectly illustrative of what it is like to live life as a disabled woman. Those two bouncers made a series of assumptions about me based on what I looked like, and felt perfectly entitled to enforce those assumptions, even when they were repeatedly told that they weren't true. That's how powerful these beliefs are – even making them consciously express their bias had no effect, so let's unpack those biases in turn.

The most blatantly absurd presumption was about what type of music I would like. As I never made it into the club, I cannot tell you what they were playing, but I'd guess it was loud and raucous, and the kind of thing you could dance to. I think the bouncer looked at me – young, blonde, a woman and a wheelchair user – and decided I must like to listen to girly pop and very sad songs. And sure, I do like cheesy pop and Adele (because who doesn't?), but I also like indie and classic rock and Motown and disco. I've even been known, when tipsy, to enjoy the odd dance track. I'm not one-dimensional, I'm not a cliché, but the bouncer clocked an electric wheelchair and a speech impediment and, in that moment, she thought she knew who I was and what music I was allowed to enjoy. More incredibly, she thought she knew me better than I know myself.

This ridiculous situation was born of deeper things, though. Disabled people, and disabled women in particular, are subject to a systematically embedded set of beliefs about which spaces we belong in.

As you read this, imagine yourself in a pub. Imagine that, when you've had a few pints, you get up to go to the loo and notice that there's a young woman sitting in an electric wheelchair, surrounded by mates and drinking a pint of cider through a straw. Are you surprised to see her? I can tell you that many people are, and I know this because they like to tell me so. 'Oh, I didn't know people like you went to the pub,' they say, or 'Well done you for getting out and about', as if it is not deeply offensive to be impressed that an adult has left their house.

Clubs, as it happens, seem to be the place where people least expect to see a disabled woman, perhaps because they are places where people go to show off their bodies and, as disabled people, we are not supposed to want to do that. We are supposed to want to hide. When I squeeze my chair onto a packed dance floor, people watch, waiting to see if I will dance or not, and quite what that dancing will look like.

All disabled people attract drunk people like moths to a flame (we're clearly just so good-looking, right?), but there is a different dynamic when you are a woman and the unwanted attention – and touching – is from leery men who want to comment on how unusual you and the workings of your body are. There is fear – will I be able to stop this man if he tries something I don't want him to? Will he understand if I say no? – but there is also a sinking feeling that, once again, my body is being seen as a curiosity. Dressed up and make-up done, as he looks me up and down, I feel my whole self being reduced to an attraction in a museum. Am I just playing a part? There is anger, too, at the rude intrusion into my night out, the reminder that no matter how much fun I am having with my friends, to someone else I am slightly less than a person. And there is shame for the fact that, for a split second, I feel myself hope that maybe he just fancies me, and for the realisation that, even if he did, I probably wouldn't believe it.

The problem is not just confined to people who are mildly inebriated. There are all sorts of places where people are surprised to see a young, female, actually-very-disabled-if-we're-being-honest wheelchair user: in the world-history section of a bookshop, in expensive restaurants, and, more than anything, trundling into work at a world-leading journalism institution. In so many situations, people catch a glimpse of me out of the corner of their eye and pause. Cock their head to the side a little; consider. And sometimes I can see their whole conception of what is possible for someone who looks like me shift, just a tad. And sometimes it does not shift at all. For that Clapham bouncer, conceptions of the possible were very rigid indeed.

This brings us to the last big old assumption she made about me: that I didn't have any power. This is where my being disabled and my being a woman combine into more than the sum of their parts. In that moment, as I struggled to make myself heard, looking up at her from my chair, I must have seemed at the mercy of her discrimination. She doubtless thought that there was nothing I could do – that I didn't have the know-how or the strength or the voice to make a fuss and create consequences for her actions. She knew the crowd wouldn't intervene, and she knew I couldn't barge my way in. I wonder if, as we turned and left, she felt a small glimmer of satisfaction that she had won this argument and got her way. I, however, knew differently.

As my friends and I headed for suitably greasy food, they fumed. 'Who do they think they are?' was uttered repeatedly, along with excessive use of the word 'outrageous' and even more profuse use of words which aren't fit to print. I nodded, trying to get a word in with these two brilliant women, but also enjoying their indignation.

'Girls!' I finally managed to say. 'I have a plan.'

What that bouncer didn't know was that I was then working at BBC *Newsnight* and had an extremely wide network of journalists, writers and campaigners in my corner. I also knew how to use Twitter. So, I went into work the following Monday, nodded along in the morning meeting, and got typing.

By the end of the day, my tweets had been seen and shared by many thousands of people. Newspapers, magazines and my very own colleagues at the BBC picked up the story, amplifying my voice at each turn. In the corridors and lifts at Broadcasting House, colleagues stopped me to express their shock and congratulate me on taking a stand. The BBC had contacted the club in question, who had promptly apologised, pledged to retrain their staff, and offered me a night on the house (shockingly, I didn't take them up on it). I went home exhausted. But I had proved that bouncer and her assumptions wrong. I had been heard.

This story of a failed night out is just an extreme example of countless instances of sexism and ableism that have shaped my life. These two forces are like a constant gale-force wind, invisible yet extremely powerful, which have slowly moulded who I am and how I interact with the world around me. I cannot remember a time when I did not feel their judgement and their attempts to limit me, and yet I'm willing to bet that while you know all about sexism, you're not so sure about ableism. Perhaps you haven't even come across the word before, which in itself says quite a lot, so let's start with a definition.

At its most basic, ableism is discrimination in favour of non-disabled people and against disabled people. It is the privileging of certain bodies and ways of living that conform to a perceived norm. It is the belief that disabled bodies or minds – and the people who have them – are inherently inferior to others, and that therefore these people should be avoided, abused, coddled, pitied. It is a rigid set of assumptions about the literal and metaphorical spaces in which disabled people do and do not belong, which are then enforced by the power of cultural, social and legal discrimination. It is built into almost all situations, making it at once a matter of personal and system-wide relations. Ultimately, it leads to (often unspoken) decisions that some lives are less valuable than others, whether that's in terms of physical access, healthcare, education, financial security or, indeed, friendship and love. If you care about equality, you should care about ableism.

And yet, as I type this, my writing software is showing me a myriad of red squiggly lines. It doesn't recognise ableism as a word. Imagine what that feels like: the discrimination you face every day does not even have a recognised name. This denial of reality makes that reality so much harder to change. Naming something is inherently powerful, and the refusal to call ableism what it is leaves disabled people chronically disempowered. It's infuriating, invalidating, incapacitating. It is the ultimate form of gaslighting.

How do I know ableism is real? Because only 52 per cent of disabled people in the UK are employed, compared to 81 per cent of non-disabled people. Because only 84 of London's 270 Tube stations are step-free. Because national newspapers have happily run headlines about disabled 'fakers' and 'shirkers' while governments have cut disability benefits and social-care budgets. Because housing developers avoid their obligations to build accessible places for people to live. Because of pervasive abuse and violence towards people with learning disabilities. Because disabled kids are regularly excluded from mainstream schools just because they don't get the support they need. And – here's the kicker – because two-thirds of Brits told disability charity Scope that they felt awkward talking to disabled people. Two-thirds.

I know ableism is real because I live it every time I leave my flat. Let's think about a typical day in the life of Lucy, pre-pandemic. I get up and leave the house. I can't get the Tube to work because, although my local station is accessible, the one in the centre of town isn't, and anyway, during rush hour people simply do not allow me the space I need to safely get on and off a train. I order a cab. Luckily for me, all London black cabs are accessible, and the drivers are usually happy enough to hop out and deploy the ramp. I am wearing a BBC pass, but when I ask to be taken to Broadcasting House or the Westminster office, the driver pauses. 'Are you sure, love?' he asks (no woman taxi driver has ever asked me this, by the way), and then we proceed to have a conversation about how impressive it is that I am a journalist. Safe in the back, where I know he can't really see me, I roll my eyes to my PA, who is looking extremely bored.

All of these shenanigans, in case you were wondering, are because of ableism – it does not have to be this way. If disabled people were valued, public transport would be accessible. If we were respected, no one would doubt that I knew where I was going.

Anyway, we get to work and navigate the overly friendly security staff. Ensconced in the office, I am in a relatively ableism-free zone, until I make a phone call to book a guest or get a quote. I start by introducing myself: 'Hello, my name is Lucy and I'm calling from the BBC—', but by the time I take a breath, they have heard my speech impediment and stopped listening. They tell me I have the wrong number and, at best, I have a few seconds to convince them to stop, hear me, and believe I am who I say I am before they hang up. It is a challenge that I sometimes win and often lose. I send a text asking them to call back, knowing that they will almost certainly still be wary when we speak again. People don't think someone who sounds like me belongs in journalism and, you guessed it, that's ableism.

A WhatsApp message arrives from a friend: 'Pub tonight?' Yes, most definitely, but it depends where. If they've already chosen a venue, I might as well call it quits now. But luckily, most of my friends know better. 'Let me see what I can find,' I reply.

I open up Google maps to triangulate. What we need is an accessible pub near an accessible Tube stop. Click, click. Ideally, I would also like it to be nice. I find one that looks promising, but a passer-by is obscuring the Street View photo and I can't see if there's a step. I scour the pub's website, but among the menu and other assorted useless information, there isn't a single thing about accessibility. This disregard for the basic needs of disabled people is, oh look, ableism. I call the pub. The phone rings and rings. Finally someone answers. 'Hello! Sorry to bother you,' I say, immediately wondering why I am sorry. 'Are you wheelchair accessible?'

Any number of things can happen now. I can be met with a simple no, and head back to Google relatively quickly. I wonder if they feel a twinge of guilt that they are discriminating against a swathe of society, but I know that ableism has convinced them that inaccessibility is just an inevitable fact of life rather than an active choice resulting in systematic exclusion.

Sometimes, they reply all-too-quickly with 'Oh, yes, of course', and I have to ask them to check that there is not in fact a step at the entrance, which they once saw a manual wheelchair user navigate, but which would leave me sitting on the pavement. Often, they are forced to admit that actually, on reflection, such a step does exist and, no, they haven't got a portable ramp. Such a ramp, by the way, would set them back £50, or the equivalent of six London glasses of wine. If they don't have a ramp, it's because they can't be bothered to have one. Oh, look, ableism again!

Even if, by some miracle, I have alighted on a step-free pub, the hassle does not end there. Next, we need to ascertain if there's a disabled loo, and if it is actually big enough for a wheelchair, me and my PA. Most often the answer to this question is a resounding no. I have fallen at the final hurdle. I return to Google. Rinse, repeat. Eventually, I find somewhere truly accessible or simply give up. 'Come to mine?' I ask my friend. I have been forced out of public life and back into the shadows, and yet I am too used to this rigmarole to feel angry; I am too tired to summon rage.

Days like this are not exceptional. Throw in a few people

staring at me, a stranger asking what is 'wrong' with me, or a waiter assuming I can't read a menu, and all you have is a typical day. This constant inaccessibility and ableism not only limits where you can go, but the experiences you can have or the life choices you can make. Ultimately, it limits who you can be. And it creates the undeniable knowledge that the world isn't made for you and doesn't want you in it; that you do not belong. Unremarkable but powerful, this is ableism – a constant current against which disabled people are forced to swim, and, to make matters worse, a current that those in calmer waters insist isn't there. It is endless, exhausting and, perhaps worst of all, still somehow socially acceptable.

Much of this ableism is faced by all disabled people, although of course exact experiences vary depending on how 'acceptable' society judges a person's impairment to be. I have an unshakeable feeling, however, that the ableism I experience is coloured and often exacerbated by sexism, and the particular mental calculations people make – consciously and unconsciously – about disabled women.

As a simple way to introduce and illustrate this point, and as I've mentioned them already, indulge me in a little rant about disabled toilets and how their rarity is, in fact, a feminist issue. While disabled men obviously need accessible loos, disabled women are disproportionately affected when denied one. Why? Well, firstly because it is possible for some wheelchair-using men to go to the loo from their chairs. But secondly, and more importantly, because women's bodies are different and we (seemingly) need to use the loo more often than men, as anyone who has ever witnessed the queues for the bathrooms at an event can testify.

In her masterpiece of a book, *Invisible Women*, Caroline Criado Perez argues that the equal-by-space but not equal-according-to-need provision of men's and women's toilets is a big equality issue, leading to discomfort, wasted time and, in some parts of the world, health and safety problems. For disabled women, though, the problem is often not unequal provision, but no provision at all. Imagine going to the theatre, or perhaps a concert, or out to dinner with friends, and simply not being able to go to the loo. Imagine a restaurant staying open with all of its women's loos out of order, or indeed being allowed to open with only urinals and no cubicles. It wouldn't be given a licence to operate, and yet establishments are allowed to open and trade without a disabled loo, no questions asked.

What does this mean in practice? It means drinking as little water as possible and always having a headache. It means nights out with friends prematurely severed because I'm desperate for the loo and have to go home. It means frequent UTIs and now permanent bladder damage as a result of holding on for too long. And for some women, as Frances Ryan reported in the *Guardian* in 2018, it means opting for catheters they don't really need, with all the associated infection risk, just to feel untethered from their homes. Once again, it means that I feel unwelcome in the world – invisible even – with my options and therefore my life limited by other people's indifference.

This should, I cannot emphasise enough, be the cause of loud and frequent outrage. Not providing an accessible bathroom is a convenient and legal way to keep disabled people, and especially disabled women, out of your establishment. It is segregation by toilet, and it should not be allowed.

Even when there is a disabled loo, the needs of women are routinely ignored. A disproportionate number of disabled bathrooms do not have a mirror. You might not think this is particularly a women's issue, but in the society that we live in, it is. I'd like the women amongst you to imagine going to the loo on a night out and not checking your hair and make-up. Everybody does it, but if you need an accessible toilet, you are denied the right to know if you've smudged your lipstick. Less light-hearted is the implicit assumption contained within not having a mirror: that disabled women do not care about their looks because we are assumed to be, and to think of ourselves as, unattractive.

More prosaically, disabled bathrooms also, more often than not, lack the sanitary bins and tampon dispensers routinely provided in the women's bathroom. This belies another set of absurd assumptions foisted upon disabled women that contort our lives and our self-perception: that we do not have sexual or reproductive capacities, that we are really still children in older bodies. It is easy to forget that disabled women have periods if you don't really think we're women at all, isn't it?

So yes, disabled men need disabled loos, but the lack of accessible bathrooms is a feminist issue, and it is just one of many ways in which being disabled and a woman combine to create unique issues and experiences. This book is about that combination, and about what it is like to spend life at this intersection, trying to make it work, while all the while the world insists that the two – being disabled and a woman – cannot co-exist. That being disabled, in some fundamental, essential sense, means we are not really women, and so we do not belong in the spaces and categories made for them.

It's not just me who thinks disabled womanhood is its own identity and that our experiences are materially different from those of disabled men and non-disabled women. The stats agree with me. According to the UN, disabled women and girls are 'at least' two to three times more likely than their non-disabled peers to be victims of violence. Globally, disabled women are less likely to be educated, employed or have access to healthcare. Human Rights Watch highlights the prevalence of forced sterilisation and abortion, and denial of sexual healthcare, as key issues facing disabled women.

The situation in the UK is also pretty dire. Whereas British disabled men faced a pay gap of 18 per cent in 2020, for disabled women the figure was a staggering 36 per cent, according to the TUC union body. For non-disabled women it was 17 per cent. The Office for National Statistics found that in 2021, disabled women were more than twice as likely (52 per cent) as non-disabled women (23 per cent) to be completely economically inactive. Disabled men do slightly better, of course, at 46 per cent.

Perhaps most starkly, UK figures from 2020 showed that disabled women under the age of sixty-five were eleven times more likely to die in the first wave of the Covid-19 pandemic than other women of the same age – and research showed that this was due to socioeconomic, rather than medical, factors.

But it's not just the big, measurable stuff. It's small, everyday but relentless instances, like not getting an invitation to your schoolmates' girly sixteenth birthday parties. Like an H&M accessible changing room full of unused mannequins. Like a boy in a student club who kisses you because his friends dared him to. Like being mocked on dating apps and always being the third wheel when your friends find partners. It's being told to be grateful that you have a job you've earned; being told that you should never have kids; being told to just be happy because you've already beaten the odds and defied the narrative you were supposed to conform to.

It's the group of young boys in oversized jeans who elbow each other to make sure they've each noticed you and the suited man who leans right over your head to get something off a supermarket shelf. It's the surprise in the checkout guy's eyes when you pay for something yourself. It's the drunk man outside a pub who demands 'a spin'. It's feeling excluded even with your closest friends. It's all the sodding pity. It's a pat on the head or, worse, a hand on your knee, because this body of yours is seen as public property. It's mentally assessing whether saying something back will make it stop, or put you in danger. All of this and so much more – this is what it's like to exist in the world as a disabled woman.

Over the years, I have become more open about my day-to-day experiences of disabled womanhood – first with friends, in my early twenties, and then, by my mid-twenties, anyone who would listen. Colleagues, carers, strangers on the internet – I started telling them these anecdotes in a desperate attempt to get people to understand that the world I inhabited was vastly different from theirs, that my experiences of womanhood were often the polar opposite of the ones they shared. Every single story I told, no matter how banal it appeared to me, was met with the same response: disbelief. Eyebrows would shoot up and, occasionally, jaws would literally drop. People could not believe that these things happened to me, in London, in the twenty-first century. And every time I would find myself saying, 'Well yes, of course! I'm disabled and a woman, what did you expect?'

I realised that what appeared obvious to me was, to others, a brand-new way of seeing the world – and that this ignorance came from a lack of visibility. Put simply, very few people had ever thought about disability in a social or political sense because very few people had ever been asked to. If they'd come across disability at all, it was in the form of an ageing relative who needed help to do the shopping. Disability was not part of their working life or how they socialised – at least not until someone like me came along to shatter the illusion. And even if someone did have a passing acquaintance with disability, no one ever seemed to have connected ableism and sexism, or to have recognised that the two were common yet antagonistic bedfellows. And who could blame them?

Disabled women are not represented – in the media; in film, TV and books; in political, cultural or economic institutions. We are largely invisible, our concerns overlooked. Body-positivity movements ignore us; clothes aren't made for us (what's with all the jumpsuits?); sex education and even sexual-health clinics exclude us; conceptions of motherhood erase us. Schools harm us, workplaces undervalue us. The dating scene is actively hostile to us. Physical spaces leave us out in the cold. We are denied a voice, denied agency, denied belonging. Often, it is denied that our dual identity – disabled/woman – exists at all.

I am a lifelong, ardent feminist and I can't remember a time when I wasn't aware of the disability rights movement. But even in these two social movements – two movements which have politically housed me for the better part of two decades – disabled women remain peripheral. This, by the way, makes no sense. Non-disabled women suffer from the ableist narrative that all bodies should be (a) similar, and (b) productive, and women are just more likely to become disabled or have a chronic condition, whether because of old age or simply from the strain of existing in a world that expects you to be taller, stronger and not pregnant.

Much feminist energy goes, rightly, into getting 'women's work' recognised as work, or to freeing women from sexualisation. All of this is undeniably good, but what about those women who can't do a lot of work, domestic or not, or whose sexuality is continually denied? Similarly, there is a focus on women being self-sufficient – emotionally, financially, physically – so that they are free from a life of relying on men, but only recently has the importance of interdependence been granted, despite disabled women knowing and living it every day. So much of the body-positivity movement is predicated on celebrating what bodies *do*, a sly but very effective way to exclude disabled women. To adapt from Hillary Clinton's famous phrase, disability issues are women's issues, yet so much of feminism is still predicated on the woman's body as an ideal – less Photoshopped, but still 'independent', productive and able.

The disability movement has its own issues. Take, for example, the classic 'accessible' symbol. A disabled man pushes a manual wheelchair without help. This act in and of itself is easier for men than for women – men just have more upper-body strength. We also know that men are less likely to have chronic or pain conditions than women, and that these conditions are more likely to fluctuate. Where is the visual representation of that? This all plays out in the campaigns people choose to wage: a lot is said about accessible transport, very little about access to sexual-health services or help for disabled parents. Almost nothing is said about domestic abuse. Even within the movement, independence can be overvalued – especially in the (much-needed) fight to be housed in the community – betraying very male attitudes to the nature of care and caring. For disabled women, then, even the movements meant to liberate can instead erase us further.

This constant silencing, this feeling of existing in a world not built for or welcoming of who you are, has an effect on all aspects of a person's life, from care to education, jobs to political views, relationships to healthcare, as this book will explore. But it also has profound effects on less visible things too: one's self-confidence, mental health and conception of who you are. For me, these internal ramifications of misogynist ableism have been just as important as their material consequences, and whilst I can't possibly convey a lifetime of discrimination, this book is an attempt at an honest account of what it is to feel these things, as well as to live them.

A lot of this book is angry. Anger is a natural response to injustice, and yet it took me so long to allow myself to feel it, so I think it is important to write the truth of it. I am angry at all the ways I have been discriminated against for being disabled, and at all the ways ableism and sexism have robbed me of choice. I am angry, most profoundly, at how disability has been weaponised to deny my womanhood, and all the exclusion I have endured because society doesn't allow me to be both. All of this is openly shared here.

But the book is also about finding joy where I am supposed to despair – in the power and kindness of care, in the solidarity of community, in my own voice. I've found joy in the ability to see humour in the absurd, and in the small moments in life I only get to experience because I happen to be disabled and a woman all at the same time. Mostly, though, I've found it in the tremendous, heart-stoppingly fierce friendships I am surrounded by, and this is a book about those, too.

So, this is a story of contradiction: one of anger and joy, anxiety and hope. It is personal and political. It is a reflection of the world as it is and a plea for it to do better. But, really, it's just a story about a young girl who was told she didn't and couldn't belong, who went out anyway, battled with the world, and found places, people and new ideas that proved she did.

So, before we dive into some of the big, thorny questions about disabled womanhood that arise from my existence, let's start with the basics.

I am Lucy, a late-twenty-something who lives in South London and firmly believes that this city is the best place on earth. Like my life, I have a penchant for contradiction. I am chatty and crack jokes and have bouts of extreme anxiety. I am a journalist by trade, a writer by nature, and I have, shall we say, the courage of my convictions. You could call me an introvert – leave me with a pile of books for a week and I will be almost surreally happy – except that I also adore the company of all the friends I can never quite believe I have, and will often be out until the small hours, laughing and drinking and dancing. I have cerebral palsy and blonde hair and a face that betrays exactly what I'm thinking. I have twenty-four-hour care and I feel completely in control of my life.

I am disabled, and a woman, and a disabled woman. I am excluded everywhere and I belong right here. What's it like to be this person? Well, let me show you.

Chapter 2
My body: Acceptance amid exclusion

Trundling down the pavement in my wheelchair, I can feel eyes on me. Usually, it's a quick glance; the stranger clocks me, looks me up and down, moves on. Every now and then, though, the glance turns into a stare. My body – the way it sits, the way it moves – is rendered a curiosity, a freak abomination. They watch as I approach a crossing, stare as I reach for the button, wonder if I'll know to look both ways. Eventually, I make it across the road without flinging myself in front of a car, and they look away, relieved. They think my body is incapable, that it is in need of a minder. I pretend not to notice.

I'm sitting in a restaurant with friends. The waiter hears us chatting and notices my speech impediment. Assuming, for some reason, that I can't read, he fails to give me a menu, and is embarrassed when I share a mate's. When the food comes, a teenager at another table watches, eyes wide, as a friend feeds me. He thinks my body is gross, my reliance on others grotesque. I pretend not to notice.

In a shop, I want to try on a dress. It's the most expensive one, and the shop assistant fails to mask her surprise. She looks awkward and apologetic when I have to ask her to empty the accessible changing room, which is full of spare clothes rails and half-mannequins. She says they don't get many disabled people in the shop, but what she is really saying is that these fancy, feminine dresses are not for me. She thinks my body does not belong here. I pretend not to notice.

I'm having a drink in a crowded bar. People dramatically throw themselves out of my way as I gently manoeuvre between the tables, turning me into a public spectacle. I smile in thanks, pretending not to notice. I cannot get my chair under the table, so I must lean awkwardly, struggling to hear the conversation, pretending not to notice that I am excluded from the circle. I cannot go to the bathroom, and two drinks in, I am pretending not to notice that I am desperate for the loo. My friends feign a conversation – they can't hear me properly over the music and noise – and I pretend not to notice that their responses don't match what I've just said. A woman I do not know comes over to tell me she doesn't see 'a lot of people like you' in bars. She tells me she feels sorry for me, that she wouldn't leave the house if she 'ended up' like me. In her eyes, I am not a woman having an after-work drink but simply a broken body, an object to be pitied. I pretend not to notice, turning away and staring into the middle distance until she walks off. A man comes over, intrigued by my wheelchair and body, and puts a hand on my knee. My body is so desexualised in his mind that he sees no problem in treating it like a piece of public property, but I am scared. I can no longer pretend not to notice.

This is what it is like to move through life in a disabled body. To exist just outside, at one remove from society. My body sticks out. It is different from the norm. This much I know and accept. What is infuriating and difficult to live with is the multiple judgements people make about this difference, and, by extension, about who I am and how they can treat me. At school, it was a source of shame, weaponised as an excuse for bullying. At the station, where requests for a ramp are met with a huff of annoyance, it is just an inconvenience. At industry events, it is a reason to doubt that I belong in the room. In matters of romance, it is reason for rejection, and in matters of parenthood it is reason for exclusion. At the doctors my body is simply a problem, an aberration of biology for which there should be – but isn't – a fix.

In all of these situations, it is assumed that my body is wrong, bad, a trap that holds me back from a good, fulfilled life. This is the message that bombards me each time I leave the house, and has done for as long as I can remember. Is it any wonder that for much of my life I believed it was true?

Like so many things, the story of my relationship with my female, disabled body – and how it has been shaped by society – begins when I was a teenager. Back then, I had a warped view in which it was my cerebral palsy that was responsible for everything bad that ever happened to me. This went along with an even more warped understanding of my own appearance. I was so preoccupied with what I couldn't do that it would have never occurred to me to even wonder if I liked my body, let alone if I liked how I looked. I had clothes I liked, sure, and hairdressers always cooed over my extremely blonde hair, but these things felt removed from me, Lucy, the person, who liked writing and hated stairs. Mostly, I was baffled every time someone mentioned my appearance; it was, after all, the least important thing about living in my body.

This meant that, remarkably, I never disliked my body in the regular teenage-girl sense. I'd never thought I was too thin or too fat, never agonised over whether my chin was a weird shape. I guess in some ways I was lucky – the TV perfume ads and the models in teen magazines struck me, even then, as faintly ridiculous, and my body was so far from those I saw in the media that I never felt compelled to compare myself. I was already, unsurprisingly, quite a fervent feminist, and I believed then, as I do now, that for the love of God you should definitely just eat the cake.

I thought this meant that I had a very healthy body image. Reader, I did not. I couldn't see it then, but now it's clear to me that I harboured a profound animosity towards this body I was living in. I was endlessly frustrated by the things I couldn't do with it. I wanted, desperately, to be able to write out those dreaded GCSE chemistry equations myself, rather than laboriously dictating them. I wanted to be able to go to the loo alone. I wanted to be able to dash up the stairs at school. If I'm honest, the thing I wanted most in the world was to be able to argue with my parents and then stomp off, slamming the front door as I left. (There were some ways in which I was still absolutely the archetypal teenage girl.) Perhaps it is important here to explain precisely what living in this body is like. Cerebral palsy, if you were wondering, is a form of brain damage that occurs at or around birth – but really, the biology isn't important. I honestly couldn't care less about *why* I can't do things, a statement with which even teenage Lucy would agree. The thing to understand is how it feels. The only way I know how to explain it is to say this: imagine that your body is one big game of Chinese whispers. My brain thinks about moving my hand, and sends the appropriate message, but then the message goes through the teeny-tiny damaged bit of my brain and comes out a bit scrambled. What I end up with is a version of the original – less smooth, more jerky, but still some approximation of what I intended. Put it another way, using my body is a bit like when you ask a toddler to put on some shoes and they reappear wearing their mother's high heels.

The consequences of this are myriad and unlistable. All of those mistranslated messages mean that some muscles are overstimulated and some never used. I am in constant movement, a puppet attached to a shaking hand. I can think of coordination, can see what needs to be done, but the movements never quite sync – a foot lifted just a split second too late to keep up with my hips. I can feel balance, know exactly when I'm going to fall, but there is nothing much to be done about it.

Some muscles and joints take the strain of all these missed connections. My right hip takes nearly all of my weight when I sit. My spine is curved. My speech is slurred. I type with my thumb, index and third fingers – the middle one refuses to move independently. I cannot pick up a mug, or undo a button, or brush my own teeth (I tried once as a small child and knocked out a milk tooth that wasn't remotely wobbly). I can stand and walk with help, sometimes even up some steps. But relinquish me completely and I will slowly tilt to one side until I am falling. I try not to imagine myself as a felled tree. This is my body. And as a teenager, I was at war with it.

Back then, I blamed my body for everything: for the fight to get to the end of the school day, exhausted and sore. For not being able to keep up with my notes in lessons and for how much longer than everyone else it took me to do my homework. I can see myself at a school desk, begging my hands to move faster, calculating what I could leave out while my peers produced folders and folders of notes. The comparison made me panic. I blamed my body, too, for having to rely – at that age when all you want is independence – on my parents to wash me, dress me, feed me, take me to the loo. I'd sit at the kitchen table and imagine getting up to make a sandwich. Once, I even tried – and watched on, infuriated, as everything I pulled from the fridge tumbled to the floor. The frustration was unbearable. This body, I thought, stopped me being who I wanted to be – the person that, deep down, I still thought I really was.

It wasn't just the physical things, either. As a teenager, in a world that told me my body was a critical flaw, I blamed it for things it was completely, wholly not responsible for. I blamed it for the social exclusion, the bullying, the boredom of being stuck at home. I blamed it for leaving me stranded whenever there was a step, and for needing the bad carer I had. I blamed it for the misery and the feeling of being trapped and the crippling fear of the future that pervaded my teenage years. Whenever the frustration boiled over or someone was particularly mean, uncontrollable tears would soon follow. I would pummel my own thighs, angry beyond words with these legs that refused to work. I wanted, with a desperation that staggers me now, to be free of this body that I saw as being so utterly broken and defective. It felt like a cage, like the only thing between me and happiness, and I would have given anything, anything at all, to make it go away. I fantasised about a life in a different body – a Freaky Friday-esque swap with one of the peers I was so jealous of. It was, if I'm honest, a very bleak way to see yourself.

One wonders if this animosity to my body would have been quite so strong if I had been a teenage boy. Would I have been so aware of my difference? I always considered myself lucky to be a girl because at least I was under no societal obligation to play sports. But looking back, I'm not so sure. Everything in our culture tells young girls they must mould their bodies to fit in, to belong, and yet that was far beyond what I was able to do. Everything tells girls to be capable, elegant and, most damagingly, unnoticed. Yet everywhere I went, people stared, and my body clashed with the physical world, making me feel like an awkward misfit, a square peg in a round hole. While I may never have bothered to wear make-up to school, I did spend a lot of time thinking up ways to look 'less disabled'. School assemblies spent trying to quell the involuntary movement of my feet led me to have what I now recognise was my first panic attack when I, of course, couldn't move them. This was a purely social concern – the movements weren't doing me any harm at all – but I felt as if the eyes of every person in the school were on me, noticing, labelling me as different. In those long years, I wanted, above anything, to disappear, to blend in so much that no one would see me at all. It never occurred to me that I just needed to be seen in the right way.

On the surface, my feminism should have been a guiding light in finding acceptance of my body. Somehow, though, my political beliefs about women's bodies never seeped into my personal beliefs about my own. The idea that your value is not bound up in your physicality but in who you are as a person – a tenet of feminism which I would have had tattooed on my arm – didn't quite translate to my reality, in which my physicality was causing me no end of grief. It all seemed like wishful thinking, designed for people living other, less physically determined, lives.

The particular brand of feminism I grew up with was particularly alienating when encountered from a body like mine. Body positivity was just starting to make a dent in the model-heavy early noughties culture, but every diktat to 'love yourself' came with a plea to focus on what your body did for you, not what it looked like. Naturally, this did little good. I thought – or had been made to think – that my body was useless, so basing my self-worth on its physical capabilities was sometimes actively bad for my conception of myself. Mostly, though, that early body positivity just seemed irrelevant and out of reach; the preserve of girls who, while thinking themselves flawed, were infinitely closer to the ideal than I would ever be. 'Why care about your weight,' I would quietly seethe, 'when you can get up the stairs?'

Then there was noughties feminism's insistence on the insignificance of the body, and its peculiar belief that women's physicalities didn't matter. (How many times were we told to fit into the world of men – 'work like a man' – rather than being encouraged to listen to our own strengths and needs?) These supposed ideals only bolstered my own deeply unhealthy tendency to deny my body attention and strip it of importance. In my head, there was an alternative Lucy, floating just on the edge of existence, who wasn't disabled – who at times didn't have a body at all. My all-consuming goal, back then, was to be as much like her as possible. In those years, I could really see her in my mind's eye, always better and always there to compare myself to. I used to frequently start sentences with the phrase: 'If I wasn't disabled, I would . . . ' Every time I dropped my phone (approximately twelve times a day) or had to ask for a glass of water, I felt I had failed to live up to this other Lucy; that my life was worse than the one I could be leading. This alternative version of myself was smart, witty, even anxious sometimes, but she was, to me, unencumbered, free. I wanted to be her, but I also resented that wanting. To think about it now makes my heart ache for all the years when I didn't realise that my body was capable of living a wonderful life; that I was not some knock-off version of a perfect self; that there is joy and love to be found in imperfection, and in truly being who you are.

This tendency to imagine a non-disabled alter ego wasn't helped by the fact that everyone else around me was in on the act. The most familiar refrain of my teenagehood was not 'Come downstairs', but rather, 'You can do anything you put your mind to.' When I protested that I had in fact put my mind to a great many things – walking, feeding myself, painting my nails – with no hint of success, people subtly changed tack, pivoting to a new argument that went something like this: 'It doesn't matter that you can't get yourself dressed, because you're smart!' This was said with the fervour of trying to cheer up a distressed fourteen-year-old when there's nothing that can be done, and I have no doubt that these kind people really believed that what they were saying was true. On some level, I think I believed it too, if only because it chimed with all this shallow feminism I wanted to believe in. Unfortunately, my already slightly neurotic brain interpreted this mantra as: it doesn't matter that you can't get yourself dressed, *as long as you're smart*. It should come as no surprise that I became quite the perfectionist.

I interpreted this potent mix of denialism and unrefined feminism as a sign that I wasn't supposed to care about my body – that my physical realities shouldn't matter, because thoughts or personalities or ideas are important, and bodies are not. I took this entreaty to ignore my body too seriously, refusing to give it what it needed or, at times, to even see it as part of myself. So, while I hid the shame of hating my body, I also became alienated from it, seeing it as irrelevant to who I was or what I was trying to be.

And then, imperceptibly at first, things started to change when I was maybe sixteen or seventeen, thanks to a new and radical (at least to me) understanding of disability itself, one that would eventually allow me to set down the self-blame and self-loathing that I'd been carrying around for so long. This understanding did not come from the flawed feminism of my youth, but from a vibrant community of disabled activists, writers and thinkers, who had been doing the work of loving their marginalised bodies for longer than I'd had one.

Many disabled people can tell you about the exact moment they discovered the social model of disability. My story is not so simple – there was no sudden illuminated lightbulb in the dark. I think this is because I first encountered it as a kid and it just didn't make a lot of sense. It took growing up – and becoming more political – to really understand the power of this single idea. It was less of a big bang and more of a slow simmer.

The social model of disability can and should transform your understanding of disability, so buckle up. Here comes the explanation of the most important idea in this book. Ready?

At its heart, the idea is this: I am disabled by ableism and inaccessibility, not by my physical impairment (aka my body). Confused? Let's put it another way. When I can't go to a pub because there's a step, I am not disabled by my inability to walk, but by the failure of said pub to provide a ramp. The more you think about it, the more this is true: if a ramp is provided, I don't gain the ability to walk, but I do gain access to the pub. My impairment hasn't changed one jot, yet I can do more. So clearly, it isn't the impairment that's causing the problem.

For a long time, I understood this as it related to stairs and inaccessible transport and the lack of disabled loos. These things evidently did prevent me from doing things I would have been able to do if access had been provided. This was as far as my understanding went, however. I couldn't see how the social model applied to the issues that really worried me: bullying, care and my future employment prospects – things that no ramp or lift could help me with.

Here's the revelation: the social model applies to all of it. Disabled kids (and adults) get bullied because their bodies are judged as less than and because the world is not built for those bodies. If I hadn't been forced to try to join in with non-disabled PE, perhaps the girls at school would have had one less thing to judge me for. Disabled people are also bullied because disability is not seen as normal – perhaps if disabled people were on TV or in magazines, they wouldn't be avoided at school. In the world of work, perhaps if we didn't equate productivity with long hours, more disabled people would be employed. Perhaps if offices were accessible, more wheelchair users would sit at boardroom tables. Perhaps if local authorities actually provided people with the care and equipment needed, disabled people would be able to work, socialise and form relationships in much the same way as everyone else.

As disability campaigner Katie Pennick once told me, everybody – and every body – has needs; it's just that society chooses to meet the needs of non-disabled people and not those of disabled people. That's the difference between a non-disabled person and me, and it's got absolutely nothing to do with one of our bodies being better than the other. If all disabled people's needs were met, being disabled wouldn't have to be associated with so many negative things. It could just be a neutral description of a person, the same as being tall or having brown hair. This is the social model in action.

Can you see it? The problems disabled people face are not created by our bodies but by society. In other words, my body is not to blame.

I wish I could say that this all came to me as some sort of epiphany, but it didn't. It took me years to absorb the truth of all this, and to see that the way I had felt about my body for the best part of a decade was a symptom of an oppressive narrative that values disabled bodies, and people, as less than their non-disabled counterparts. In reality, bodies don't have inherent values (except as things that very kindly allow us to be alive). Mine is simply one that the world is not built for.

Taking the social model to heart radically changed how I saw the world. If the fault was with society, that meant things could change – or be changed. And, slowly, it meant I could stop being so mean to myself.

The changes were small at first. I stopped hiding in the corners of rooms, trying to blend into the walls. I stopped wishing I sat straighter when I looked in the mirror. I stopped trying to still my feet, accepting instead that they will wiggle of their own accord and people will just have to ignore them.

And then the shift accelerated. At university, after a stern talking-to from a friend, I finally stopped saying 'Sorry' every time someone opened a door for me, got me a drink or helped me with my coat. Soon after, I stopped apologising when we had to change plans for nights out because of stairs and inaccessible loos. I took a big step in the summer of my second year when I turned down a work-experience placement because it was inaccessible – this from a girl who, during her A-levels, had enlisted her dad to carry her up and down several flights of stairs to a magazine's offices every day for two whole weeks, just so she could sit around doing next to nothing. And what do you know? The more I expressed what I needed, the less what I needed seemed like a big deal. I accepted that there were just some things I couldn't do and so I became happier in my own skin. Confidence seeped into me like a warm bed after a cold walk home. Eventually, I was not at war with this body of mine.

The social model and disability advocacy gave me a framework through which to understand disability and redirect my anger and frustration away from my body and towards an inaccessible, ableist world. It also allowed me to accept that bodies do matter, because the ways in which they are or aren't accepted and accommodated shape how our lives turn out. Acknowledging this isn't a failure to be a real feminist, as I once believed; it's instead a prerequisite of anti-ableism and living a good female, disabled life.

The social model allowed me to begin to challenge all the crappy things that I had once attributed to my body, and to see them for what they truly are. Still, having this knowledge deep in my bones does not make navigating disabled life easy. Mostly, this is because other people still think of disabled bodies as the problem, conveniently absolving themselves of any responsibility to do anything about ableism and inaccessibility, which they take as the natural state of affairs. In fact, sometimes the gulf between my understanding of disability (as socially created) and everyone else's (where it is immutable) is itself a source of maddening frustration. If only they could see the world as I do, we could actually create change.

The stark contrast between my internal acceptance of my

body and the world's obvious discomfort with it can make holding onto the former feel like an uphill battle. It is a continual mental exercise to remember that all bodies are good bodies when people so often assume mine is bad, or when they refuse to accommodate it at even the most basic level.

Inaccessibility in particular wears away at my hard-won body acceptance. I can know full well that access is a societal problem, not a 'me' problem, but that does nothing to change the fact that living in an inaccessible world is bad for your mental health. The constant hassle of getting around problems, checking access and being forced to change plans is draining in itself, but it is nothing compared to the pervasive knowledge that you and your body are deemed unworthy of consideration, that people are happy to exclude you without a second thought. Inaccessibility is a choice – and that choice is to render a large and diverse group of people second-class citizens based solely on their bodies. It is the ultimate form of judgement, of saying: you do not belong here. That judgement, no matter how much I know better, can still sting, leaving the bitter taste of adrenaline in my mouth as I am stranded yet again – yet again – at the bottom of a flight of stairs.

The world is simply not built for bodies like mine. Every outing is a reminder. Every phone call to find out whether I am afforded the right of freedom of movement is another affront. When, in the course of a single day, repeated instances of inaccessibility bleed into each other, it is hard not to feel that you simply do not fit, your body at odds with the physical environment. Sitting outside an inaccessible shop your friend has dashed into for you, craning to see the sandwich options while getting wet in the rain, frustration and anger are only natural. One has to hold one's dignity tightly lest it slips away.

There are certain areas of life that, for one reason or

another, are particularly inaccessible – hospitality, travel, the entertainment industry. This is not just deeply frustrating but it also actively limits your choices about where you can go, which people you can meet and who you can be. A sterile chain restaurant is infinitely more likely to be step-free than a family-run place, and in some parts of London the only place I can have a drink and use the loo is a Wetherspoons. Forget trying out the latest pop-up cocktail bar or seeing an up-and-coming band in a small venue. Forget getting last-minute tickets to a play or stumbling upon a comedy gig. Spontaneity is only possible if the world is designed for you to move through it with ease, hardly noticing all the small ways in which you are accommodated.

There are also specifically feminised spaces that remain inaccessible. I was once tasked with organising a friend's hen-do, only to find, as I suspected, that all the spa or pampering places were off-limits. Many hair salons and nail places and so on are inaccessible, and even the ones where you can get in are often impossible to navigate, filled with fixed stools and too-low tables, leaving nowhere to sit in a wheelchair. Nice clothes shops and little boutiques are often too narrow, and people just love to use accessible changing rooms as storage areas. Using these spaces is, obviously, not a mark of womanhood, but being excluded from femininity can feel invalidating when you do, in fact, identify with it. Sometimes I just want to be girly.

Inaccessibility can also have more serious repercussions for disabled women. We often can't access vital services: sexual-health clinics and maternity wards do not have the hoists to allow disabled women onto examination beds. The inaccessibility of these services can mean some women go without the medical care they need, or at the very least foster the feeling that these spaces are not for us (more of that later).

Inaccessibility can also be physically dangerous for disabled women. Inaccessible public transport can leave us walking home late at night. Difficult-to-navigate public and social spaces can make it impossible to get away from leery or harassing men. At the most distressing level, the abject lack of accessible women's refuges can trap disabled women in abusive relationships. Even if, by good fortune, you never experience any of these situations, the knowledge that you could means you've always got an eye out for an accessible escape route. The world's refusal to accommodate our disabled female bodies can thus make living in one feel like running the gauntlet.

If inaccessibility is a choice, it is clear that we could choose access. We could choose to include disabled people in general, or disabled women in particular, but we don't. In other words, it does not have to be this way. It stays this way because society judges disabled bodies as less than. This is a depressing thing to face when you're just trying to buy some T-shirts.

What's worse, though, than the long-ago choice not to build a ramp, are the in-the-moment and right-in-front-of-my-face decisions to use my body as a reason to be an ableist arsehole, like assuming I can't read, or asking my friend if I'm actually able to pay for dinner. Almost all of these decisions are driven by three related ideas about disabled bodies: that they are failures, that they are disgusting and that they are objects of pity.

The pity is what gets to me. It's there in the assumption people frequently make that simply because my body doesn't work like theirs, my life must be a mixture of boring and tragic. That I cannot possibly have a fulfilling job, or good friends, or indeed anything to be happy about. That my body is a cage, trapping any potential or aspirations I may have once had. 'What a shame,' they say. 'That poor girl.' It's there, too, in the presupposition that I would give anything, do anything, to be 'cured' of this terrible affliction – they never consider that it would be fairly odd to want to be cured of being yourself – and that my life must be one long, futile quest for the magic elixir that would make me whole, functional, 'normal' again. It's not hard to see where this belief comes from: every film and book and article has convinced them that using a wheelchair is a fate worse than death. Indeed, they tell me that in my place they'd kill themselves.

Because this pity leads to all the other discrimination I face, I have no choice but to spend my days convincing random strangers that my life is worth living. I feel compelled to share stories from work just to stop them cocking their heads at me in *faux* concern. I say, over and over and over again, that 'disabled' isn't a bad word; calling out every gross euphemism – 'differently abled,' 'special needs' – that implies otherwise. I use my distinctive voice and I literally take up a lot of space. I fling my arms around on the dance floor. I post selfies on Instagram. I wear bright colours because I refuse to do as expected and hide. I refuse to be ashamed.

The truth is, I am proud of my body. It not only exists but thrives in a world that isn't built for it, and it confounds expectations at every turn. I do not buy into society's bullshit laws that say disabled bodies cannot be loved and cherished, or that disability and beauty cannot coexist, or that disability precludes happiness. I know now that there is nothing 'wrong' with my body, and I no longer compare it to a hypothetical non-disabled form of itself. It is not a knock-off version of a perfect self. All bodies are good bodies – not because all bodies look good or work well, but because all bodies are part of the people they belong to, and because without them, we simply wouldn't be here. As a proud disabled woman, I know that my body has just as much value as anyone's.

The thing is, though, that the constant need to insist that disability isn't a bad thing can make it hard to admit when you are struggling with your disabled, female body, as I found in my early twenties when, after a few heady years of enjoying my body, things started to get harder again. At this point, I was still clinging on to my proto-feminist-inspired belief that my body didn't matter, which was not ideal when it turned out to matter a great deal. I had, let's be clear, fully accepted that there were physical things I couldn't do. It had been years since I'd given any serious consideration to my inability to walk, feed myself or take myself to the loo. I had achieved a Buddha-like zen about this stuff. I frankly no longer cared. What I hadn't wrapped my head around, though, was that being disabled was going to affect more than how I moved around. It was going to affect how I lived.

By the time I was twenty-two, I was working ten-hour shifts on the BBC News UK online desk, sometimes getting up at 6.30 a.m. for whole days of pushing my un-cooperative hands up to the speed required for breaking news. A few months in, I was in agony, a dull haze of pain clouding my thoughts. My back, which spent the whole day tightened so I could have more control over my arms, no longer recovered overnight. My shoulders became tighter and tighter too, taking on the extra strain of holding my head up properly in the office (it's harder than it looks). My back frequently felt as if someone had taken a lighter to my spine; a kind of searing pain that made it hard to think straight. I was surviving on Deep Heat and increasingly strong painkillers. The day I took half a codeine tablet at work, I was so spaced out that I remember desperately hoping there wouldn't be any Cabinet resignations. I was pushing my body too far – and I didn't know how to tell anyone in case the admission was taken as evidence I couldn't do my job. I suffered in silence for months, slowly making myself sick.

It is incredibly difficult to like a body that hurts. This shouldn't be a revelatory sentence, and yet it feels like one. When your back is throbbing, it is hard to remember everything you know about feminism or the social model of disability. Indeed, sometimes it is hard to remember anything much at all. Forget excelling at work, you're just trying to grit your teeth through the pain. Sharing a laugh with colleagues is out of the question when all of your energy is focused on trying to keep the discomfort off your face. Staying after-hours to finish a story you're really invested in becomes impossible when you're counting down the minutes until your shift is over. If you have to leave early, God forbid, you can forget having a sense of achievement; you can only feel disappointment and worry for your career prospects. Any instinct that you may have had to be kind to your body is sorely tested when your body is being anything but kind to you. It feels like a personal affront; a punishment; a tribulation to be borne because you have dared to aim too high. It feels as if your body is letting you down. It feels like it's once again stopping you from being yourself.

All of this, I think you'll understand, made it quite hard to fully embrace the feminist imperative to 'love yourself'. Indeed, I'm sure the very fact of being a woman made this harder. Women are so often held to a standard of perfection that we eventually begin to hold ourselves to it. When I was battling through a day at work, sore and tired and increasingly unable to keep up, I felt very far from perfect. I felt like I was failing. The idea that I was a modern woman in charge of my own success seemed simply laughable. My body seemed to be the one in control.

Of course, now that I'm out the other side, I can see the whole episode differently. My body wasn't failing me, social norms around productivity and presenteeism were – as were the strictures of a certain kind of feminism that implored women to work, well, like men. There was absolutely no reason why, as an online writer, I needed to be in the office, but we lacked a computer system to allow working from home. I had also internalised a lot of external pressure that meant I felt unable to ask for shorter shifts. While this refusal to seek alternative working arrangements came from me, it didn't originate with me, but rather from a culture that equated time in the office with productivity, and that saw showing up as a key part of doing your job. A culture that made working about as inaccessible as it could possibly be. We treated all of this as if it was inevitable, the only way to do business. And then the pandemic happened and turned working practices upside down overnight. Suddenly, showing up and being productive were uncoupled. Working from home became the norm. The way we worked changed, to allow for people's personal circumstances, whether that was home-schooling or dropping off shopping for a shielding relative. The world had shown that when it wanted to change – when non-disabled people needed it to – no one claimed it couldn't be done or that things had to be the way they were (all things disabled people had been told by employers for years). This meant that, for the first time in a long time, I felt like I was on a level playing field when it came to work. I was still in pain, but I could manage it. I was no longer ill with exhaustion. I could do my work well. Lo and behold, once again it wasn't my body that had been the problem, but the way society is structured. I chalked up another victory for the social model.

How had I strayed so far from the social model and fallen into old habits of blaming my body for things beyond its control? Surely, part of the problem was that no one around me talked about these issues from a social-model perspective, making it all too easy for me to slip out of it too. My pain was seen as an immutable fact – if I mentioned it, I was just given the day off – rather than something to accommodate, and so that was how I started to treat it, too. I'd been taught all my life, by a woefully un-intersectional girl-boss feminism and the people around me, to ignore my body – to believe that I could 'overcome' its physical realities with sheer force of will. But the pain I experienced at work forced me to confront my body, to learn to meet it where it is. The social model and the pandemic had taught me that it was possible to meet my physical needs alongside my intellectual ones. So I looked around, assessed those needs, and made the decision to go freelance. And when I stopped fighting my disabled body, stopped ignoring it and instead looked after it, I found it a hell of a lot easier to like. Finally, what I knew about the value of disabled bodies and what I felt about mine were one and the same.

Still, I haven't exactly got it all figured out. My relationship with my body is continually knocked off its delicate equilibrium by new challenges and new encounters with ableism, particularly the tortuous ways it interacts with sexism and my identity as a woman. Indeed, one of the trickiest and most difficult things to deal with is people's constant refusal to see me as a 'proper' woman, whatever the hell that is.

One of the many reasons that this is difficult to handle is that it's hard to explain. There is no explicit denial of womanhood that I can point to that would show you what I mean. Instead, it's a slow accumulation of side-eyes, slights and unspoken messages. Of course, the physical inaccessibility of women's spaces plays a significant role here. Femininity, like lots of social identities, is created in groups, and when you can't physically access the places where these groups congregate, exclusion is inevitable. But it's more than a physical problem. It is a failure of our very conceptions of femininity and womanhood to include disabled women at all. Despite modern society's stated belief that womanhood can be as varied and inclusive as manhood, being disabled (particularly visibly or intellectually disabled) seems to push people like me out of the societal understanding of what it is to be a 'real' woman, leaving us outside many of the associated social spaces and identities we may wish to belong to. We become sexless and genderless, while somehow still 'woman enough' to be subjected to constant, rampant sexism. This dichotomy and its many ramifications are at the core of many, if not all, of the most painful experiences in my life.

It's important to clarify that when I talk about womanhood here, I am, for the sake of simplicity, talking about a socially recognised form of femininity, which lots of people choose to reject. Indeed, I personally find a lot of traditional femininity extremely alienating. But what's different for disabled women is that we're excluded from even the bits of femininity we would actually like to adopt for ourselves, and denied the choice to express ourselves in traditionally feminine ways when we want to.

This is often noticeable in the absences. From my supposedly 'feminist' school's failure to mention disability in several years of sex education, to my GP's failure to ask me about contraception. From the clinical, masculine design of most adaptive clothing (and wheelchairs!) to the invisibility of disabled women in glossy mags. I have seen a million and one articles with advice for girls about their first period – not a single one mentioned how to talk to carers about it. The list goes on and on. Have you ever encountered a mother and baby class that doesn't require being able to sit on the floor? What about a make-up brand making adaptive brushes?

Disabled women's bodies are so invisible that it would be easy to believe that the two categories don't overlap. I have often found traditionally feminine spaces and modes of self-expression alienating, and it has taken me a while to find a way to integrate these two key parts of my identity. For a long time, the perceived tension between them determined the choices I made about how I presented myself, especially when it came to clothes.

Societal pressures radically affected what I thought I could or should wear. Of course, there's practical considerations: can I comfortably sit in these trousers for nine hours? Do I have to be standing to do up the zip on this dress? Often, clothes haven't been designed with long-term sitting in mind. And there are questions of how easy things are to use; try getting on a pair of skinny jeans with no stretch in them with a carer. On the other hand, the limited availability of adaptive clothes often does not allow for individual style. But there are also ways I use clothes in order to mitigate some of the sexist ableism that comes my way. See here my absolute loathing of anything that could be considered 'cute'. Woe betide anyone who suggests I wear anything involving frills or suchlike. In the never-ending battle to be treated as an adult, anything too girly would simply give an advantage to the opposing side, at once stifling my chance to express my femininity and betraying how society still views all young women, disabled or not, as less than. I don't necessarily want to let these prejudiced assumptions affect my choices, but I also want to make my life easier. So I shun pastel colours, ruffles of any kind, or certain kinds of floral prints. I can't even properly define the problem; I just know it when I see it. Some of these clothes I actually like, but nevertheless, suggest an offending item to me in Zara and my nose will wrinkle in instant rejection.

In all honesty, it's quite difficult to have cerebral palsy like mine and feel feminine. Strappy dresses are out, as is any pretence at elegance. My propensity to spill things rules out anything white (if I ever do get married, catch me in blue). I must always, always wear socks, to help circulation and avoid blisters; strappy sandals and pumps are a no go. My hair rubs against my wheelchair's headrest and becomes static and messy, giving me a somewhat dishevelled look no matter how hard I try to look put together. And I have to look put together, because a failure to do so just confirms biases that disabled people can't really look after ourselves. Combine that with the intense pressure on women to look and dress uber-professionally just to be taken seriously, and there's no sloppy chic for me. An astute friend once observed that I've always dressed as if I'm older than I am, and I had to explain that it's an unconscious attempt to claw back some respect. Once again, disabled women's choices are limited by society's failure to account for our bodies, leading to a situation in which being disabled and being a woman appear to be mutually exclusive.

Having a limited choice of clothing, while an important issue, pales in comparison to other choices about our bodies which we don't get to make. Around the world, disabled women face higher rates of domestic and sexual abuse,[1] and even forced sterilisation. We are routinely excluded from sexual-health initiatives and women's empowerment programmes. Even in the UK, very little support exists for disabled mums, leading women to 'choose' not to have children when in reality it is no choice at all. Disabled women who live in institutionalised care settings – and even those who don't – are denied basic choices over how they wash,

---

1 According to a 2017 UN Women report, disabled women are at 'three times greater risk of rape, are twice as likely to be survivors of domestic violence and other forms of gender-based violence and are likely to experience abuse over a longer period and with more severe injuries' than non-disabled women.

dress, eat and go out, and almost all of them are denied sexual agency, either by care staff or by a society that sees them as desexualised and infantile.

Indeed, desexualisation is the most profound way in which my womanhood is denied. It's quite an odd experience to be in your twenties and treated like a sexless automaton, a core part of yourself stripped away. I am assumed to be either completely uninterested in or actually incapable of having sex (neither of these are true), often by people who are otherwise comfortable with disability. I have been desexualised for so long and so often that it is actually hard to pick out specific moments that can adequately convey the strength of this messaging, but nevertheless a few spring to mind: someone at school asking me if I really needed to go to our sex ed lesson. Friends cutting short conversations about university one-night stands when I joined the chat. The GP who assumed I wanted to go on the pill just to control my periods (I was twenty). The countless times someone on a dating app has told me they won't date disabled women because they 'like sex' and we, apparently, don't.

Because people think my body is 'sexless', they feel able to treat it as public property, as an oddity to be explored. Not only do they feel entitled to ask about it – including its sexual capacities – they often feel entitled to touch me, in ways that can be gross or invasive or even scary. Often, it's a hand left too long on my arm, or a creepy stroke of my face, but not infrequently it's a hand on my knee or, worse, my lap. To me, because I conceive of myself as a sexual being, this obviously feels frighteningly sexual, but what's really horrifying is that they don't see it like that at all. When a friend screamed at a man in a pub in Dublin for having his hand on my thigh, he was almost as appalled by the idea he looked like he was hitting on me as I was by the invasion.

In these circumstances, it becomes difficult to acknowledge or understand your own sexuality. There is no model for asserting your sexual needs, especially as, at the other end of the spectrum, some disabled women are hypersexualised by fetishists and those who find perceived vulnerability to be a turn-on. The constant insistence that you simply cannot be a sexual being makes it easier, sometimes, to deny that part of yourself to yourself, and feeds the feeling that you are not quite a real woman.

Even when it's not related to desexualisation, being the subject of this refusal to see disabled female bodies as women's bodies inevitably affects your sense of your own womanhood, leaving you feeling alienated from your own sexual and gender identities. How could it not, when it's so constant and insistent? Mainstream feminism, with its focus on bodies that move through the world in typical ways, offers no help here, and nor, on the surface, does the disability rights movement, which often ignores the particular ways female disabled bodies are doubly marginalised. But as I've got older and applied the social model more fully, I found myself wondering if it might not hold the beginnings of an answer not just on disability, but on disabled womanhood, too. If disability is a social construct, then so too must be the notion that being disabled makes me less of a woman. And if that's true, I can choose to disregard what society tells me about my womanhood and what it means for where I belong, in the same way I have learned that my body is not at fault for its own exclusion.

For the past few years, then, I have attempted to treat my disabled, female body with something approaching compassion. I have, finally and wholeheartedly, stopped blaming it for exclusion, instead seeing that it is ableism and inaccessibility that leave me socially and physically out in the cold. I have also forgiven myself for the ways I castigated and ignored my body, instead understanding that I was made to do so by a society that saw it as broken and pitiful. I now treat my body with kindness, even on the days when it most clashes with the world that is not built for it, even on the days when I am left squirming in pain by a society that demands too much. The social model now sits at the heart of everything I do, a thick armour that allows me to tackle the world's injustices without constantly subjecting myself to the wounds it tries to inflict.

Belatedly but joyously, I have also taken a bold new step: I am reclaiming womanhood and femininity for myself. I am wearing what I like (usually a bright pink pair of Doc Marten boots), regardless of what others think. I am exploring my sexuality – finding freedom, self-expression and parts of myself that had been locked away. I am discovering feminine spaces and modes of expression that feel right for me and not worrying about whether others agree, because I know who I am and they do not. These days, when I look in the mirror, I like what I see, because I see a disabled woman, fully and completely. And I finally feel like one, too. In doing so, I have reconciled myself to my body. We are no longer alienated from each other but one and the same. I belong to it, and it belongs to me.

Still, progress and emotions are never linear, and no matter how strongly I believe that my body is not at fault and my womanhood is not in doubt, the world continues to tell me otherwise. It still refuses to meet my needs and it still excludes me, physically and socially, every single day. What I know about myself is difficult to hold on to when I am once again stranded by the absence of a lift or when someone turns away from me in disgust. The truth is that knowing my body is worthy of belonging does not protect me from the pain of having that belonging denied at every turn. It is not enough for my feelings towards myself to have changed. How the world reacts to my body must change, too.

Chapter 3

Care:
The radical
case for
interdependence

I rely on carers for everything. I use the word 'rely' on purpose, because it's the only appropriate word. Without help, I would be completely stuck. I wouldn't be able to get up, get dressed or wash. I wouldn't be able to go to the loo, brush my teeth or tie my hair up. I wouldn't be able to cook, eat or get a glass of water. I wouldn't be able to get in or out of any of my wheelchairs, which means I wouldn't be able to move. You could forget going outside, popping to the shop, going to see a friend or getting to work. Writing would be a pipe dream because I wouldn't be able to fetch my laptop or open it. And pretty quickly I'd be unable to communicate with the outside world at all, because my phone would die and I wouldn't be able to plug it in.

So, I need a lot of help. And because I am no longer seven years old and would quite like to live my own life, thank you very much, that means I employ carers, instead of relying on my mum and dad, who, incidentally, have lives of their own, too – who knew? Carers who are employed to work in people's homes and enable them to live independently are called personal assistants, or PAs, to highlight that they are there to assist, rather than 'look after' the person in question. In conversations with strangers or colleagues or men I fancy, I try to remember to call my PAs 'PAs', because I am continuously trying to prove myself a vaguely competent adult, and unfortunately, I know that the word 'carer' conjures all sorts of mental images in their minds that do not apply. In my head, though, and when I talk to my friends, I do call them carers, because that is what they are: people who provide my care – and there's nothing wrong with that. With my family and closest friends, I refer to them simply as 'my girls', reflecting the camaraderie and support that comes from being surrounded by a group of brilliant women. Here, I am going to call them all three of these terms, and trust that you, lovely reader, can leave your assumptions about care here, at this sentence, and hear what I have to say about what care means for me.

In the past few years, the UK media has woken up to the 'care crisis'. But for all of the hundreds of thousands of words spent discussing funding, staffing and whether or not elderly people – and it's worth noting that those being spoken about in these settings are always elderly, rather than disabled – deserve basic dignity, we never get to hear from people who actually have care about what that experience is like. As a result, we've settled on an understanding of care that could not be further from the truth: that it is something depressing; a sign of failure; and something that happens to you, hopefully, for as short a time as possible before you die.

So, here's the first thing you need to know: care is great. That list of things at the beginning of the chapter that I can't do without help? Well, I can do them because I do have help. Isn't that great? Let's look at all the choices I get to make in a single, average day because I have carers, and let's talk about what such a day actually looks like, rather than whatever grim image you may have in your mind.

It starts with a soft knock on my bedroom door. My girls are kind enough to be gentle with me, knowing that there's every chance I haven't slept much and might not be ready to face the day.

The door creaks open: 'Morning! Ready for me?'

'Not really,' I mumble. 'Come back in ten minutes.'

They know I am going to say this, but every morning they are cheerfully accepting of my inability to get out of bed. They return, knock again and come into my room as I reluctantly roll over. They smile at me.

I'm groggy, so I use single words to indicate what I want to wear.

'Jeans. Converse. Jumper.'

I lift my feet so they can slide my trousers on, and then I lift my bum so they can pull them up. It's not graceful, but it does have a simple, pleasing effectiveness. We don't talk; we don't need to. Trousers and shoes on, they take my hand, and I use their steadying arm to pull myself up until I'm sitting on the side of the bed. I'm vaguely awake now, and say 'Good morning' again, laughing at my own grumpiness. A top is forced over my head, and then they stand me up, spin me round – a two-person pirouette – and plop me down in my little manual chair. We've pressed 'go' on the day.

I scoot myself into the bathroom, where they help me to the loo, brush my teeth, wash my face and tackle my spectacular bed-head hair. All of this is done on autopilot; if we do chat, it's about what I'm doing that day, or the weird dream they had during the night. If I'm going out with friends or have an important meeting, they'll do my make-up, too. I can't do any of this stuff myself, but within twenty minutes of waking up, I am ready for whatever the day holds, comfortable in my chair and looking exactly how I want to look. Isn't that something?

Mercifully, as I answer emails and read the news, they make me a cup of much-needed coffee. Then I'm left to my own devices, free to get on with work – or procrastination – until I need a hand again, with the loo or maybe something to eat. This time spent being left alone is very important; I need so much help that it would be easy to spend my entire life in someone else's company. It's also important to me, personally, to separate what I can, and, importantly, want to do for myself and what I can't. Work is my independent space – just me, my brain and a laptop.

Other things, though, I could technically do for myself but choose not to, either to conserve energy, preserve dignity or simply so I have more flexibility. Eating is a prime example of this. If someone were to cut up my food and hand me a fork, I could theoretically get the stuff into my gob, but I would end up both extremely messy and still hungry, as a not insignificant portion of my meal would end up on the floor or in my hair (don't ask). I'd be tired and frustrated, and I would be limited to only eating foodstuffs that respond well to being stabbed with a fork – forget sandwiches or salads or anything in a sauce. So, I choose to have help, to give myself the freedom to munch whatever it is I want and to conserve the energy to go and see my mates at the pub instead. This care, then, is not a defeat at all, but instead, a radical act of prioritising my own decisions. Counter to the mainstream obsession with independence, my reliance on help is not limiting; it is the very condition of freedom. And for me, it is the very condition necessary to wolf down a mountain of sushi.

Alongside the flawed belief that care is bad and a condition of unhealthy dependence, there is also a misconception that care is just about going to the loo or getting dressed or eating – in other words, that it exists solely to meet basic physical needs. This is, frankly, a lie. Good care – real care – is about enabling a disabled person to live life on their own terms. My PAs don't just feed me; they set up my laptop so I can work. They don't just shower me; they keep the flat clean and tidy and do all my washing. They don't just cook; they come with me to do my food shopping so I can actually decide what I want in the fridge. Their ability to know exactly which chocolate bar it is that I'm vaguely pointing at in Tesco is an underrated skill. Perhaps most significantly, without someone getting me up and presentable and then piling into a cab to the office with me, I would never have been able to have my job at the BBC, and I certainly wouldn't be writing this book. These are the kinds of things carers allow disabled people to do.

Work done for the day, we get ready and head to the local

pub, sometimes just the two of us, but more often than not to meet one of my friends. It is my PAs who enable me to have a social life, coming with me wherever I go, like a more useful shadow. This is a skill in itself. Good PAs are adept at reading the room, knowing when to hang back and give me space, and when I need them by my side (holding a drink). In these situations, my PAs are not there just to move me around; they also get me a G&T, hunt down a straw at the bottom of my handbag, and, like all women, know the difference between the silent look that says 'I need the loo,' and the one that says, 'This man is a creep.' They are my access to fun and friends and everything life has to offer. Theatre, comedy, fancy restaurants or drunken KFC – we experience these things as a duo, building a life that is rich and fulfilling and only possible because we've teamed up to live it. Having them beside me empowers me to make decisions and try new things, because, out in the world, it is my PAs who most often help me navigate the weirdness of ableism: ringing up pubs to check accessibility or stepping in to separate me from a drunk person who wants to know what's 'wrong' with me. They are part-carer, part-bodyguard, and with them beside me I can have the confidence to reply: 'Nothing, what the hell is wrong with you?', turn back to my mates and buy another round.

Eventually, we head home. They feed me Pringles in the back of the cab. We're merry. In these moments, I am glad not to be going back to an empty flat, grateful for the companionship and the laughter. We head to bed, gossiping about the good-looking guy in the pub so much that it takes an age to get undressed and showered and into bed. We barely notice what we're doing, so used to the routine and each other that sometimes, once the lights are out, I wonder if I did in fact take my tablets or wash my face. They pull the covers up, hand me a book, and ask what time I want to be woken tomorrow. They know I'll need my ten minutes in the morning. And then we'll do it all again.

A lot of care is intangible. It is them knowing when I am anxious because my muscles have tensed, and knowing the small things that can help. It is fitting in with my friends, becoming one with our big, rowdy group, but understanding that they are my friends and to leave us alone when necessary. It is seeing that I can't reach the TV remote and moving it closer before I ask, or filling up my drink without disturbing me while I write. It is knowing when I'm uncomfortable and what to do about it. Knowing when to be fun and when to be serious. Knowing when to help and when to let me try. Knowing when to just follow routine and when to ask. It is being the only non-disabled people who really know what my life is like, who see every instance of extra effort and every passing moment of discrimination, and who know when enough is enough. It is never judging. It is understanding the exhaustion and frustration and joy that come from being alive and disabled and a woman all at the same time.

Care is a service, and, rightly, it is paid for. Professionalism is important. You want people to know what they're doing and to take it seriously. It is also extremely skilled, requiring not just practical know-how but social awareness and bucketloads of empathy too. You have to be able to anticipate someone's needs without ever presuming, to be a reassuring presence whilst knowing when to remain in the background. It's important to recognise just how hard it is to be a good carer, and there is much to be said about how little they are valued by our society.

This is not to say that care can't go wrong or that it's always plain sailing. Managing my care is, by far, the hardest thing about being disabled. It requires a lot of upkeep – like a beautiful old house that may keel over and off its foundations at any given time. I imagine myself with a ladder and a bucket of cement, patching it up before the rain gets in to rot the floorboards. Just when one gap is fixed, another hole threatens to open up.

Most of the time, the issues are relatively minor and easily solved. Someone needs a day off, someone else covers. I am lucky to have a bunch of friends and ex-PAs who are happy to help out when they can, and, somehow, someone is nearly always available. When finding cover is straightforward, days off barely register as a problem; they're just a minor addition to the constant background noise of disability admin. The issue isn't so much that sorting it out is particularly difficult, rather that one finds oneself wondering what else you could do with your life if you didn't spend a fair proportion of it staring at a rota. (I like to think that I'd have written the next great literary sensation and become the Anne Tyler of South London. Obviously.) More stressful is when someone is sick – there is no advance warning of the flu. The call goes out on WhatsApp, but of course, unlike me, most of my friends have real jobs and are already on their way to work. We see if anyone could come later, if the person already on shift can stay longer, if we can hodgepodge together a day of care to avoid the thing I most desperately do not want to do: call my parents and cancel everything I had planned for that day or week.

Let me stress here that this is not because I don't want to see my parents. Trust me when I tell you that I see them all the time. It is not even because they struggle to do my care; they're among the best at it. It is simply because I am too old for this shit. I can't go to work with my mum, or meet my friends at the pub with my dad. The embarrassment would kill me. In the past few years, though, I've come to understand that the cause of my aversion runs deeper than that. Having to call my parents feels like failure. No matter how many times I tell myself that other grown-ups rely on their parents for all sorts of things, and that this is hardly my fault, I feel like I've failed to fly the nest. All the systems and failsafes I have built to maintain my autonomy have come to nought. What is the point of so much effort? It feels like all the other trappings of adulthood that I successfully navigate don't mean anything when compared to the fact that sometimes I still need my mum and dad to, well, keep me alive. It's not even the actual fact of it; if I go out with them for the day, I don't think twice about them helping me. It's about the lack of choice, the paucity of good options, and it's about what it symbolises: how disability keeps you tethered to childhood long after it should be a distant, rosy memory.

The other thing I struggle to get my head around is being people's boss. I am a young woman who writes things on the internet for a living – I never set out to also be an entire HR department. It's hard, at home on the sofa at the end of the day, to tell the people you live with and rely on that they're not quite pulling their weight or that you just don't like the meal they've cooked you. Sometimes the power balance feels off, like I'm supposed to be in charge but really I'm not – something that was even harder to manage when I was a very young adult and my PAs were older and more experienced in care than I was. Thankfully, I am now more confident and articulate in expressing what I want – and expecting it – but there are still countless moments when I either have to find the will to say something, or silently compromise yet again. I'm used to it, and it's life, but it is another part of the mental load of disability that is almost never discussed. It can be incredibly lonely.

All these little problems wear down your resilience for when big things go wrong. And in care, big things go wrong all the time. Sometimes, a new PA seems like a good fit at the interview but quickly reveals themselves not to be. These are the moments in which the isolation of care can become unbearable; it is so much lonelier to be essentially stuck with someone awkward, patronising or controlling than it is to be alone. I usually love the warm camaraderie of the flat, but when it becomes forced, I find being in my own space profoundly alienating. There is something about the intimacy of having an employee in your own home that makes a shitty PA so much worse than a shitty office colleague. I start struggling to do things myself, rather than asking for help, and long-forgotten frustration grows anew. From bitter experience, I know these situations are irredeemable and untenable – if it's not working now, it never will – and yet I drag them out far longer than I should because I know that when I eventually pull the plug and let someone go, life will be completely consumed by the mad scramble to find a replacement. Frankly, sometimes I do not want to cancel plans, do not want to call my parents, do not want my existence to once again be dominated by my need for care – so I just put up with dirty dishes and awful silences and uncomfortable showers until I can put up with it no more. And then, with grim inevitability, it is back to recruiting I go.

The truth is that even the best PAs leave. That's just life. They may feel like family, but they're doing a job, and people change jobs. It's no one's fault, but it's horrible. There's no point pretending otherwise. That seamless day I described? That only comes from knowing someone almost as well as you know yourself. Each of us must know the other's rhythms. With someone new, everything – from how long to leave the conditioner in my hair to how I like my coffee – needs to be explained. Nothing can be assumed, there is no routine to fall back on. Each tiny moment of the day must be narrated and explained. Each day becomes slower, requiring more physical and mental energy, so that something as simple as choosing a pair of shoes becomes just another exhausting task. New PAs take time to adjust to my speech, so each act of asking becomes itself more laborious. Precious energy – and patience – drains away. And, no matter how similarly I explain things, each new PA does things ever so slightly differently, from how they hold me to how they feed me and how much input they need from me, so as they learn my everyday life, I have to relearn it with them.

It's not just the practical stuff that makes changing carers hard. I live with these girls. We are intertwined, physically and emotionally, in each others' lives. They know if I am having a bad day, and often have an idea why before I do. They know when I'm in pain, can see when fatigue hits, and are often the only ones to see the countless small moments of ableist sexism that I don't share with my other friends. They know when I need a rest, or when I'm anxious, or when I just need a pat on the back. There is an intimacy that comes from sharing so much of your life with someone that goes past the bounds of normal friendship into a deeper relationship; we are there for each other's best and worst moments – there is no hiding grief or heartbreak – but also for all the mundane ones, the decisions about what to have for dinner and what to watch on Netflix. Much like a relationship, you build a life with someone, but, unlike in a relationship, there is no recognised way to mourn that life when someone moves on. There are no cultural reference points, no social understanding, that allows other people to understand how you feel. You're not really permitted to feel sorry for yourself when a PA leaves, and no one comes round with a tub of ice cream or a bottle of wine. People don't check in. You are expected to carry on as usual, as if nothing has changed, when, in fact, you feel completely destabilised – unmoored from a life that outwardly looks exactly the same. You find yourself, once again, living with a stranger.

Finding that stranger, too, is difficult work. Good carers – the ones who anticipate your needs and make you feel more, rather than less, confident – are an extremely rare breed. The seemingly endless cycles of recruitment blur together: CVs that are always the same, interviews where the questions are meaningless (what could I possibly ask to know how you'll deal with a sleepless night or an ableist taxi driver or a high-end journalism function?), and trial shifts that tell me nothing. Each time, the agency sends me someone who treats me like a child and, as I make excuses to end the interview, I feel anger bubbling away, covering the real emotion: fear. Fear that I just won't find someone, or that I'll hire the wrong person. Fear that they'll come and go within three months. Fear that this instability is going to define the rest of my life.

When you're recruiting, everything else stops. Forget planning for a holiday – you often can't book flights without the passengers' names – or a party on what could be an uncovered shift. Once CVs start coming in, it's hard to agree to meet a friend next weekend, because that might be the only time a candidate is available for an interview. There are so many emails. Emotionally, too, it's taxing, because each time you meet someone, you have to find a balance between openness and being guarded. Is the person sitting opposite you in Costa going to be someone you spend the next two or three years with? Will they be reliable? Will they treat you with respect? Do you like them enough to even bother trying, or should you keep looking, prolonging this endless saga? Then there's the question of how to present yourself – too stern, and they might not want the job, too friendly and they'll never listen properly again. I've had full-time care for a decade now, and I'm not sure I'm any closer to answering these questions or to making the recruitment process any less stressful. Each cycle of hiring and training, I spend months with my hackles slightly raised and my chest tight, trying to carry on as usual, while simultaneously feeling completely at sea. Sometimes it feels as though the periods where I am truly living are just interludes in the constant search, each cycle bleeding into the next. Sometimes I wish I could be free of it all; I google robot carers, but know deep down that a machine could never do the job. I try to remember that, in the end, the stress and emotional turmoil of looking are worth the result – finding someone good, and with them the ability to live as I choose – but it is never easy. It is hard. It is always hard. But there is, frankly, no other way.

So care is good. And it's also a very stressful, emotionally taxing, complicated part of my disabled female life. I love what it allows me to do. I hate having to find and organise it. I love the relationships it fosters. I hate having to start them. I think this is because, in the everyday-ness of it, my brain can fool itself that I simply live with friends who give me a hand, and that is, after all, what friends do. But when someone is sick and I need emergency cover, or when a PA moves on and I need someone new, I am reminded that I am fully, completely dependent on relative strangers. I am reminded of the hassle and effort required just so I can live. I am reminded that, for a disabled person like me, stability is only ever an illusion; one blink and it's gone. And I am reminded that all of this will be true for the rest of my days.

Reliance is a funny thing, and how I feel about it has changed dramatically over the years. Of course, as a teenager who hated her disabled body, the fact that I had to have so much help enraged me. At that age, all you want is to slip the bounds of childhood, and yet as my peers began sneaking out to parties, I still needed to ask to go to the loo. It is hard to rebel when you can't open the front door. This longing for freedom coincided, with spectacularly good timing, with needing more help than I had as a child. It was no longer physically possible, nor socially acceptable, to get around by crawling. I became ashamed of the mess I made when I fed myself, so I stopped. My secondary school was naturally bigger than my primary one, so suddenly I needed someone to push me between lessons. I kept having to ask for things, and every time I asked I felt like I was failing – failing to grow up, failing to manage, failing to cope. I was desperate for independence, even as I could feel it slipping away. I was incandescent at the unfairness of it all. I can still taste the metallic hatred I had whenever my peers opened up a new frontier of independence and I remained static. Watching them all head out after school while I headed home because my carer's shift was finishing, it was the first time I'd ever truly been jealous of someone just because they weren't disabled and I was. If my body felt like a trap, my care needs were the lock and key.

As a teenage girl, too, there was the abject horror of sharing a body I had not yet grown into. Shame mixed with fury. When all I wanted was to hide away, I was always on show. Suddenly, I needed help changing a sanitary pad. I needed to devise a way to get a bra on – a situation that somehow seemed uniquely embarrassing at the time. Teenagers need privacy in order to work out who they are and how they belong in their bodies, but nothing in my life was private. I felt vulnerable and exposed. With carers almost twice my age, I felt both pressure to grow up in order to fit into their world, and simultaneously completely infantilised, my evolving needs ignored because it was easier for everyone to pretend I was still a child. No one ever talked to me about how my care needs could mesh with having a (hypothetical) boyfriend, or about when I wanted to be left alone. Looking back, it's clear to me that I was twelve years old for six years. And then, suddenly, I was eighteen.

When I started thinking about university, a deep terror bubbled up. I was going to have to become independent from my parents, which meant having carers not only in the day but around-the-clock. It would require building and maintaining relationships not with one person but a whole team – a team made up of complete strangers – whilst also being 100 miles away from the only people who knew what I needed. I coped with this fear by denying to myself that any of it was actually going to happen, so much so that when it did, I was completely unprepared. That first weekend at Warwick, alone with people I barely knew, I sobbed and sobbed, too scared to even articulate the fear. Allowing someone to do your care is more an act of faith than of delegation; you are trusting someone with absolute control of your health and well-being without any knowledge of whether they deserve that trust. I already knew, by then, how wrong it could go; a short-lived experience with a bullying carer had left an imprint on my impressionable mind. Having to trust four people not much older than I was to perform all the tasks my parents had always done was a huge leap, a rupture slightly too big for my brain to handle. I'd strained for independence for so long, but unlike my peers, I'd received it all in the space of a weekend. It was too much all at once.

And then, four days in, I realised: this was freedom. Here was what I'd been longing for. I could do exactly as I pleased, as and when I wanted to, without consulting or negotiating with Mum and Dad. Shower in the middle of the day? Sure. Go to the pub at a moment's notice? No problem. Go to bed at 2 a.m. and get up at midday? Up to you. There was no need to squeeze in a shower when Dad got home, no rush to get things done before a carer-less weekend. I was giddy with the possibilities. I ate a lot of cake for breakfast and made up for the lost years of my teenagehood with many small acts of rebellion – chief among them, not going to any of my 9 a.m. political-economy lectures. This was the first inkling I had that care could be enabling, and my first taste of adulthood. I was a bird uncaged.

Still, I found it hard to navigate. It was difficult, at eighteen, to be someone's boss. I struggled to say when I didn't like how something was being done. I avoided awkward conversations even at the cost of my own well-being, not saying anything when one embarrassed me in front of my new friends. I didn't know how to speak up for myself or put my foot down. The care was good, and I was having fun, and I began to insist that I didn't care that I needed help, when actually I cared a great deal. People allowed me to live with this delusion despite the fact that I prefaced every request with a 'sorry'; that I apologised profusely when they had to help me with something I assumed they thought was 'gross', and that I continued to make my own life infinitely harder by insisting I could do things I quite blatantly couldn't. I was literally paying people to help me and yet I still didn't want to be a burden.

The upshot of all this was that I allowed people to make decisions for and about me in a way that I definitely shouldn't have, and in a strange way, in doing so, I made myself even more dependent on the very people I was scared to rely on. It was easier, back then, to allow someone to influence what I wore or what I ate than it was to consciously tell them what I wanted. This is not to say that they bossed me around; they were always careful to ask me what I wanted and to listen if I answered. Rather, I constantly asked for their opinions and suggestions, and then followed them blindly. This, I believed, made me likeable – and if they liked me, they would treat me well.

I loved my team, and at university I was happy, but every time something happened – a minor disagreement, a call-in-sick, a notice handed in – I felt as if the facade of my independence crumbled to dust. Each problem was a reminder that I relied on these people to be able to do any of the things I was doing. I felt precarious, balanced on top of a wobbly tower of other people's whims, a tightrope walker who could be knocked down with any hint of turbulence. Being a boss at eighteen felt overwhelming and unfair – a responsibility I'd never asked for – which made it hard to assert that I was in charge and even harder to decide whether to allow another shift swap or not. I said yes to everything. I wanted to be able to do all of this myself, to learn how to live and make my own mistakes without worrying whether the person in front of me was having a decent time at work. The truth is, even though I was desperate for the freedom that full-time care gave me, I was woefully unprepared for the responsibility of managing it. And because I thought, as one does at eighteen, that I should have it all figured out, I didn't really ask for help and spent a lot of time convinced I was failing. My care was letting me live a life that only a few years before would have seemed impossible, and for that I was grateful. But deep down, I still resented that I needed it at all.

I struggled even more with accepting help from people who weren't my carers but helped because they liked me – a concept I simply could not fathom at the time. A conversation with Becky, still one of my best friends all these years later, stands out in my mind: arriving for a chat over coffee and cake, I apologised for asking her to help me with my coat, and she roundly told me off for being an idiot. I was promptly banned from apologising. As ever, she was right. Slowly, I began to allow my new friends to do more for me: to grab me a straw from the bar, kick a chair out the way and, yes, wrestle my coat off me. Gradually, it occurred to me that in these female friendships, the giving of care was the giving of love. This seed of understanding would later help to transform my understanding of what it is to rely on people, and I am forever grateful to Becky, and the rest of my beloved Warwick crew, for showing me that.

Right up until my mid-twenties, care felt less like something done for me than something that happened to me. I felt I had no choice but to surrender myself to other people's rhythms, and to be as undemanding as possible: to never ask for any more than absolutely and strictly necessary. I lived a utilitarian life – a fact I only realised when someone talked of the shower as a time to relax and reset, to treat your body with kindness, and I was surprised to learn that you were not required to be in and out in the shortest possible time. During the Covid lockdowns, with time to think and life shrunk down to within four walls, I started asking for little things I'd never asked for before – moisturiser after a shower, a candle lit, a bookshelf rearranged into a logical order rather than haphazardly stacked. These were minor requests, barely noticed by the PAs who fulfilled them, but to me they represented something new: putting myself and my wishes first, and knowing that I deserved help not just to survive and work and socialise, but to enjoy a quiet night on the sofa, and to live with as much choice as anyone else. When new carers started, I imposed from day one that I was to be asked and listened to, that I was the one making decisions. I have even (mostly) stopped apologising when I ask for things. This has meant that the quality of care has improved, and so I am less frustrated by my continued reliance on other people. It's still hard when things go wrong, but I do not feel like a burden any more. Not one little bit.

How much of this journey has been influenced by being a woman? I think, if anything, asking for help is even harder for men – they feel they should be tough and self-reliant in a way that women don't. Just look at how many men struggle to ask for help with their mental health. Anecdotally, too, I see this in action: my male disabled friends consistently refuse offers of a helping hand, even for extremely minor things. Asking for help may be easier for women, then, but I think the societal pressure on us to be likeable can make it hard to ask for that help to be good, or to really express what it is we want. I know from my own experience that an ingrained need to be palatable and unobtrusive makes it incredibly hard to say when you don't like something, or to assert yourself when someone else is taking control that should rightfully be yours.

I also believe that, because disabled women in particular are so often assumed to be weak and vulnerable, we put pressure on ourselves to be the exact opposite. We have to portray ourselves as stronger and more independent than we really are so that we are not taken advantage of. This self-imposed hard exterior can make it particularly hard to admit when you are tired and need help with something you could do yesterday, or to choose not to do something yourself because it isn't worth the effort. You feel you ought to try, so that you're only relying on others when you really have no other option.

Recently, though, I have been asking myself why we place such a high value on what is quite a stereotypically masculine, even macho, understanding of reliance as bad. After all, everyone who's ever been a parent knows that it takes a village to raise a child. As a society, we have pretty arbitrary notions of when needing help is and isn't acceptable. It's fine to outsource your cooking and cleaning, but not feeding or washing. Why? What makes one an efficient use of time and money and the other an abject failure? Is it, perhaps, that non-disabled people are allowed to need help without being deemed a burden, whereas disabled people are not? From where I'm sitting, it sure as hell looks like it. And if that's true, isn't the most radical position one in which I am not ashamed but in fact proud of my ability to say 'help me', as and when I chose?

What's strange is that independence is valorised not just by the mainstream but by those who ought to know better. Feminism's icons are held up as 'strong, independent women'. We are all familiar with the pillars of 'girl-boss' feminism – the idolisation of women, often entrepreneurs, who turn themselves, and only themselves, into marketable brands, and the myth that they did so single-handedly. The fetishisation of independence is there in the appeals to 'be your own boss', to 'think like a man' and to 'put yourself first' – that is, in the feminism that dominates our cultural understanding of equality. Once again, disabled women are left out of the conversation, unable to reach this one-dimensional ideal.

Lots of disability activism, too, is predicated on arguing that disabled people are not needy or should be enabled to be as 'independent' as possible. I always feel a twinge of unease when I see a disabled activist rail against the assumption that they need help, because underneath the understandable hatred of assumptions, there's a deeper feeling that help is failure and that to need help makes you what no disabled person wants to be: vulnerable. You see it in the reluctance of people – even those who claim to be 'proudly disabled' – to ask for help even if that help would vastly and unarguably improve their lives. As someone who has never had a choice but to rely on others, it is odd that a movement so dedicated to the normalisation of access needs can be remarkably silent on personal ones. What message does this send to those of us who never could choose whether to ask for help or who need it the most, who, because of biological and social factors, are more likely than not to be women?

Nevertheless, I think these movements hold the beginnings

of new ways to talk about reliance. Indeed, on the fringes, they always have. As the young feminists of today start to reject the extremes of individualism, and understand its relationship to capitalism's most toxic elements, I am reminded of the first- and second-wave feminists who dreamed of women's communes, of communities where needs were met and people nurtured to be their full selves. These feminists, now and in the past, recognised that no one is truly independent; even the most fit among us relies on the village of humanity to feed us, educate us, keep us healthy and meet our emotional needs. Not a single person is their own farmer, teacher, doctor and friend. No woman is an island. Neither should we aspire to be; it is the relationships that bind us that create the richness of the human experience.

The truth is that despite all the struggles involved in having care, I cannot imagine life without these women. Nor would I ever want to. There's something uniquely close about these relationships. And I think it's important to recognise that the bond is made particularly strong because we're all women. My male disabled friends certainly do not have the same relationship with their (often female) carers, but I can't imagine it any other way. There is a natural openness in my PA relationships because it isn't awkward to talk about periods or ask them to readjust my bra, which, over time, builds easiness around tougher subjects like mental health, ableism, sex, or, indeed, the meaning of care itself. I have been able to ask questions and get to know myself in all sorts of ways because I'm able to be honest – honest to a degree that isn't really possible with anyone else.

These conversations have been invaluable in creating the confidence I have today. And while my girls accept that they can't know what life as a disabled woman is like, every woman has faced the unfair assumptions that go with living in the patriarchy. That shared experience means they can empathise with my experiences of ableism, especially as they often experience it with me in real time. In short, I am forever glad for the power of women's friendship, and the extra support that comes from spending life nestled in a team of women. There is nothing more empowering than knowing the person standing beside you in a crowd of strangers would go into battle with you if asked. It's a bit like having your own personal, very small and extremely friendly army.

It's nevertheless important to recognise the alarmingly gendered nature of the care industry. According to the King's Fund, a leading health think tank, around 80 per cent of social-care staff are women. This is a huge disparity. The fact that care work is assumed to be women's work makes it extremely difficult for disabled men to find the male carers they would understandably prefer, which makes recruiting carers one of the few things that is easier for disabled women. But it also makes conditions worse for the women who do this vital work.

The pernicious presumption that care comes naturally to women – that we're somehow just made to help others – means that training and education is often rudimentary and sometimes not fit for purpose. This is bad for both the carers and the people being cared for. In reality, as we've already discussed, care is highly skilled. I can't help but think that if more men were carers, the industry would have long ago undergone the professionalisation we've seen in nursing and other such fields.

And of course, (women's) care work is quite literally undervalued. The average hourly pay for a care worker in the social sector is just £9. Carers are often required to travel between multiple clients in one shift, but don't get paid for the time when they're driving. Many are on exploitative zero-hours contracts. Think back to all the things my girls have done for me, experienced with me and taught me, and then ask yourself if people who do similar work – often in tougher circumstances – don't deserve decent pay and conditions.

I see the continued undervaluing of carers in the way some people, especially men, treat my PAs. When I worked in an office, I had colleagues who would have been outraged if someone had discriminated against me, but who never so much as acknowledged the presence of the very people who made it possible for me to be there. It also shows up when my girls attempt to advocate for me. So often, when one of them tries to complain about inaccessibility or call out ableism, I watch as they're completely dismissed – by men, but also by other women. Occasionally, a male friend or my dad will intervene and the difference in respect is extraordinary to witness. In some sense, it is as if the carers themselves are subject to vicarious ableism; by being women associated with disability, they are treated in much the same way as I am as a disabled woman.

This should be a huge feminist issue. We rightly hear so much about the pay gap in more traditionally 'professional' industries, and a lot about the unpaid labour women do at home. But we hear so little about the vital, life-sustaining but often thankless work done by hundreds of thousands of women in the care sector. It's time for feminism to give them a voice, too.

This is one area where the feminist and the disability rights movements should be working in tandem. Better conditions for the women who work in care would obviously mean better care for those who need it. We all benefit if carers are less harried, better trained and better paid. Most importantly, we as disabled people want carers who have chosen this work for positive reasons – to help people have good and fulfilling lives – not as a last resort. Change requires lots of money, but we know what's needed.

If I could do one thing to change society, it would be redesigning the care system from scratch, overnight. But sadly, no one seems to want to give me unbridled political power and an unlimited pot of cash (unbelievable, I know). So what I can do, and what you can do, is change how we talk about care, so that politicians and the public start to recognise how important it is. If we started valuing care and carers, we'd be halfway there.

So please remember: being cared for is no tragedy. Anyone who sees me and my girls out for a meal or a trip to the shops ought to be able to see that. They ought to be able to see that care is life-enabling, not the terrible thing that happens to you at the end of an otherwise well-lived life, but instead, for some of us, what makes such a well-lived life possible. It is not the nasty failure of a broken body; not a clinical reduction of a person to their physical needs. It is simply the receipt of help to live life as you please, with dignity and choice and autonomy. And whilst it is a service, it feels, to me, much less like when you pay for a meal or a haircut and much more like when a woman silently offers you a sanitary pad at the bathroom sinks. It is communal, supportive, an act of acknowledging a need and meeting it simply because that is what everyone deserves. It is, indeed, caring.

After all these years of muddling through, I can see my relationships with my PAs in a new and kinder light. Most obviously, while I rely on them for physical help, they rely on me for a predictable pay cheque. But the interdependence is also less prosaic: as often as I ask their advice, they seek out mine. We each have our skills and something different to offer: they help me choose an outfit, I help with the studies many of them pursue alongside their work. We open up worlds for each other – where they may introduce me to new social circles, I can give them access to professional ones. Emotionally, too, the support goes both ways. As many times as we may discuss my work anxieties, we'll talk about their relationships. I rely on them, and they rely on me. We are, like everyone, interdependent. There is nothing to be ashamed of for any of us.

Despite this hard-won understanding of the true nature of reliance and independence, sometimes I still struggle to apply the abstract to my real, day-to-day life. My relationship to these concepts is still slippery, still changeable. To this day, how I feel can change with the circumstances of my care. When care is good, I am secure in my need for it – happy to receive the help and the possibilities it brings. When things fall apart, my whole life is knocked off-balance. Is there a contradiction in my love for my care and my hatred of its upkeep? Yes. Do I still struggle to reconcile myself and my fiery nature to my absolute and total reliance on others? Yes. But there is no road map here, just hard-won lessons. And if I know anything now that I didn't before, it is this: needing and giving help are essential parts of what it means to be free.

Chapter 4

Making friends: What does it mean to fit in?

My PAs have always been among the few people who make me feel rooted in the world. They create a sense of having a place, when elsewhere I so rarely feel that I fit in. I wonder if this is a common experience for disabled women. We exist in what feels like an upside-down, inside-out universe, our triumphs and challenges and place in the world often the exact inverse of those of our closest friends. We exist at one-space-removed. There's a gap between what I have learned about how the world operates and how the people I love assume it does, and sometimes that gap can make me feel crazy, like I have imagined everything I know to be true. No amount of explaining can bridge the divide because even though my friends believe me, the lived experience of disability is not a belief but a visceral knowing, a sense deep in your chest that you are not quite of the society you find yourself in. You are separate. Apart. In her memoir *Easy Beauty*, philosopher Chloe Cooper Jones writes of how, as a disabled woman, she has mentally survived by leaning into the divide between herself and the rest of the world. It's a feeling I've tried and failed to name for as long as I can remember; a sense of being of the world and yet not fully part of it, of being separated – physically, but also existentially, in some ephemeral sense.

I feel this most often when I find myself as the only disabled person in a room – whether that room is one full of acquaintances, colleagues or beloved friends. At some point before I was conscious of it, I became aware that I was different. It's a piece of knowledge so ingrained in me that I cannot conceive of not knowing it, one that has been reinforced and remade by every raised eyebrow and awkward pause when I introduce myself or say something apparently unexpected. I can be part of a group of colleagues or friends, integral to its make-up, but still, when it comes to non-disabled people, I am always demarcated. Always different.

I don't know who I would be if I fitted in. After all these years, being an outsider has become central to my sense of self. This is hard to explain when you have spent your life surrounded by people who love you. How can you so clearly have a place among them and yet feel so totally apart? It is one of the many contradictions involved in the question of disability, womanhood and belonging. Other contradictions: do I feel different because I *am* different, or because I am treated as such? Do I really want to belong, or have I been conditioned to want it? Do I want you to celebrate my differences or ignore them? And if they were universally accepted, would my entire understanding of myself crumble in the space taken up by my exclusion? What does it mean, really, to fit in?

As a child, I knew that there were things I couldn't do, and these things made me different. I also knew, from very early on, that the way the world treated me was about more than my physical abilities. I could see the tentative approach, the flicker of fear behind their eyes, the overstretched smiles of people who treated me like a toddler even when I was seven or eight. What's remarkable is that I don't remember being upset by any of this. Annoyed, yes; angry, sometimes; but not sad. I was completely sure of the fact that the problem lay with them, that they were ignorant and silly, and that I could win them over to the cause of normalising disability with a cheeky grin and a joke. Most of the time, as a child, this worked.

Until, all of a sudden, it didn't. I can pinpoint the exact moment in my life when knowing I was different morphed into knowing that I was being excluded: the week in Year 8 when we were supposed to do a sponsored walk round Richmond Park. We'd been tasked with splitting ourselves into groups, which we had to submit to our form teacher so she knew that no one was walking alone. As the week wore on, I remained groupless. Eventually, I plucked up the courage one break time to ask a group that included a few of the girls who could, on some days, be nice to me. To this day, I wish I had just left it, because I can still hear the words directed at me by another one of the group: 'Why would we want to do a walk with someone who literally can't walk?' she said, half laughing, half sneering. I could feel the words pass through me, a physical weight crushing any breath I could have used to respond. The other girls shifted uncomfortably, but no one spoke up for me. I spluttered something incomprehensible and wheeled away, feeling my conception of myself shift beneath me. A new hatred for who I was took hold. I was twelve years old.

By the time the bell had gone for the next lesson, I was in the hallway, unable to get my breath through wracking sobs. This is how my carer found me, a look of confused concern spreading across her face. Eventually, she would become used to this scenario: leaving me somewhere for a lesson or lunch time, relatively content, only to return and find me in acute distress. One nasty comment or humiliation after another stripped me of the confidence and happiness I had grown up with. I developed a nervous twitch as I tried to shrink myself away, to put a brave face on the despair growing like an inflated balloon in the space where my lungs had been. The horror of bullying repeated itself over and over again, until I woke each morning with a knot in my stomach, and spent each day coiled with dread, waiting for the next wound to be inflicted.

How do I convey to you what seven years of bullying does to a teenage mind? Perhaps it is best to simply paint the scenes most etched into my mind. Years of science lessons in which the teacher would add me, an awkward third wheel, to an already-formed pair for experiments, because no one wanted to be my partner. The empty desk between where I sat and the rest of the class. Walking along the corridor with a group – a moment of acceptance! – only for them to peel off down a flight of stairs and leave me stranded, waiting for an adult to stop and open the door to the lift, no one even bothering to look back over their shoulder to notice. They were careful, always, to make these slights seem accidental. No one ever called me names and, at a posh girls' school, no one would have dreamed of getting into a shouting match, let alone a punching one. This was a respectable kind of bullying, the kind that makes you wonder if you're just imagining it, if you've gone completely mad. The kind that makes it impossible to report to teachers, or to even say if it was done intentionally, and that leaves you wondering if this is just the natural order of things. I found myself, for the first time ever, wishing that I could be someone else, desperate to be more like the very people who were causing such misery. I became a stranger to myself. I came to believe that being disabled meant being alone, doubting your place in the world along with your own sanity.

There were some instances when the intention to be hurtful was clear, which was horrid at the time but somehow now makes me feel better because I can be sure I didn't imagine it all. One of their favourite tricks was to be friendly during school hours, but make clear I was not welcome in their social lives. This went on for the entire seven years of my secondary-school education; a particular cruelty that played on my insecurities and left me grateful for scraps of attention. I finally realised exactly what was going on one break-time in the sixth-form common room. I was perched in my wheelchair at the edge of a group of my so-called friends. The rest of them were spread over the sofas, making no effort to make space for me to get closer. Still, at least I was part of the conversation. They were making plans for their respective eighteenth-birthday celebrations, deciding between house parties or fancier affairs.

One girl, who had spent years being an on-again-off-again friend, went round the circle, checking that everyone could make a proposed date for her birthday bash. And then, she simply skipped me. Just like that. A casual cruelty, a small humiliation to go along with the litany of small humiliations I had endured at that school. I wasn't even shocked. But I finally knew that I would never be accepted by these people, that they would never be my friends. I resolved to get my A-levels, finish school, and never see any of them again.

Looking back, it's the brazenness of the cruelty that stands out. So long as I was doing well academically, the school didn't care, and the girls knew it. I was completely alone. To this day, I wonder if the fact that I went to a very competitive school made a difference, if only because there was such a premium placed on perfection, and in their eyes I was obviously and intrinsically imperfect. I didn't stand a chance. But more even than the high-achieving nature of the place, I think what really mattered was that it was a *girls'* school.

Teenage girls are primed to want to fit in. It is their reason for being. From books about best friends helping each other ask out cute boys, to films about girl gangs who navigate the perils of high school together, every piece of culture marketed at teenage girls drums home the importance of having friends. And not just any old friends, but friends who like what you like, do what you do and, especially in the mid-noughties era of my youth, look how you look. There are two priorities: being 'in' with your chosen group, and keeping everyone else out. Is it any surprise that the film I most heard quoted wasn't *Harry Potter* or *Twilight,* but *Mean Girls*?

And the thing is, I didn't fit in. Not one little bit. Not only did I definitely not look like them, I didn't have a life that was anything like theirs. I wasn't able to head out for a mooch around the shops after school. I couldn't participate in the drama, music or arts clubs that helped them develop their interests and personalities. Even if I had been invited to parties, I wouldn't have had anyone to take me, and I was too ashamed to have my dad drop me off. They were starting to get interested in the guys from the boys' school – and later came dating and boyfriends and suchlike – but this was a world beyond what I could dream of. I made up crushes so that I could take part in these giggly chats, but I could feel the distance between my life and theirs. I was an outsider, my nose pressed against the window of the teenage lives unfolding around me.

What would it have meant to have had diverse stories – ones that celebrated our differences? Would it have been better for me, and countless others like me, if the films we watched and the books we read had involved disabled teenagers? If disabled characters were on the Disney Channel going to parties and kissing boys? If E4 (I'm showing my age here) had a disabled presenter introducing their endless reruns of *Friends*? I truly believe that it would have made a world of difference, not only for me, but also for the girls around me, if representation had been there, an example set. Why was it so lacking? Teen culture then was much more homogeneous than it is now – just think back to the speed at which certain clothing brands became the 'it' thing. Feminism, which the school and pupils preached but did not practise, hadn't yet gone intersectional. When I talk now, as an adult, about the importance of media diversity, I am speaking for my teenage self, for what she desperately needed and never got.

For a long time afterwards, I blamed the girls I went to school with for what I thought they had done to me: destroyed my confidence, twisted my very understanding of friendship, and, by the end, left me absolutely convinced that I would be lonely for the rest of my life. During those seven long years, I started to hate being disabled in a way that I never had as a child, and I blamed them for turning me into such a person. Now, though, with a few more years of adulthood behind me, I no longer hold them responsible. They were under enormous pressure to fit in and be perfect because they were teenage girls at a school that revelled in its impossible standards. My anger has instead shifted towards the school, to the teachers, who could have intervened but didn't. The school, who could have made the case for difference, or at least for basic kindness, but didn't. The school, which could have ensured I wasn't put in humiliating situations, but, repeatedly, didn't (a school trip to an adventure playground looms large in my memory). Yes, this is where my anger lies because they were a huge, powerful, apparently renowned institution, and I was a twelve-year-old girl.

Sometimes I wonder if they just assumed that the situation was inevitable. Maybe the thinking was that I was the only disabled kid, so of course I was going to be left out. Maybe they just didn't care. I don't know. But the decision not to intervene and to let me struggle on alone has had ramifications for years after the bullying was over. I spent the next decade unable to believe that I really belonged in any group of friends – no matter the evidence to the contrary – and I was inherently sceptical of new people. I was fixated on the idea that people were nice to me because they had to be, not because they liked me. I was never quite convinced that my friends today would be my friends tomorrow. Outer confidence hid a veritable smorgasbord of insecurities; keeping them all hidden behind a smile fuelled crippling anxiety. The ripple effects of that time kept coming, rolling into each other until the waves threatened to swallow me up. I saw myself as a misfit, believing that I would always stand out and apart. It would take me years to unlearn the conviction that being disabled meant being alone, and even then, that fear would rear its head again whenever things got tough. This is what seven years of bullying can do to a person. And yet, despite what I believed, I was about to find a place where I did belong – and eventually, I'd start to believe it.

I am sitting in a lecture hall, feeling a little awkward about the fact that I am right at the front. Everyone else is filling up the seats at the back, but this is where the wheelchair space is, so this is where I have to sit. I must appear incredibly keen. I can feel myself going a bit red as I consider how this must look. But just as I start to get anxious, Becky arrives, spots me and heads over, grimacing at the title on the lecturer's PowerPoint. She sits down beside me, our easy chat starting where we left off yesterday. Our friend Alex joins us, and then another Becky, and then Josh too, and soon the whole front row is full. We are six weeks into our first term at Warwick University and suddenly, miraculously, I am learning what it is like to have mates.

The people here are different. I spend the vast majority of each day popping in and out of my flatmates' rooms, ignoring my seminar reading. My phone pings with invitations to the pub or a night out or a society social. People cheerily introduce themselves as we wait for seminar tutors or check out books from the library (most of which go unread). When I remember to call my mum, it is to marvel at the basic but new-to-me truth that most people are, well, nice. Becky becomes my friend in week one because, in our first seminar together, she repeats, verbatim, a point I have made, making sure I get the credit. It annoys her that the tutor hasn't understood me. We have never met before, but I decide that she's a keeper. Within weeks, we are singing along wildly to the Backstreet Boys at the campus nineties night. It takes all of three days for my flatmates and I to know each other inside out (thanks in no small part to tipsy games of truth or dare).

I can barely comprehend the speed at which life has

changed. I have never had so much fun. I pretend to study, but hungrily accept invitations to every single campus event. No one has mentioned disability in a negative way, and certainly no one has purposefully excluded me. Everyone I meet takes the time to understand my speech. People get in touch to check if the club in town is accessible before they book tickets. I can feel the tension flowing out of my body. For the first time in a long time, I sleep at night. For the first time in a long time, I am happy. For the first time in a long time, I do not hate being disabled.

I was undoubtedly extremely lucky with the people I met during those first few weeks – and the next few years. But it's important to recognise that my ability to fully participate in university life was not a random stroke of good fortune. Warwick's campus, in stark contrast to my school's, was completely accessible: not only step-free, but full of automatic doors and dotted with disabled loos (even if people did use the one in the students' union for, er, extra-curricular activities). My wheelchair could fit under the tables in the campus pub, I could reach things in the library and, crucially, walk the same route as all of my friends between lecture halls. Not a single path ended without a dropped kerb. Access allows you to participate. But so does a culture of inclusion. Because of its accessibility, Warwick was the first choice for lots of disabled students. Here is a lesson for the wider world: accommodate disabled people and we will come. This meant that every request I made for an adjustment – whether to my bathroom in halls or to the spread of my essay deadlines – had been heard and accommodated before. It made me feel comfortable being myself in a way I'd never experienced. On a basic level, too, seeing disabled people around campus – even occasionally having to queue for a lift! – let me breathe more easily. I cannot overstate what a difference it makes not to be the only visibly disabled person in a space – and I wasn't even the only visibly disabled person in my flat. That feeling of being the odd one out, which had set itself in my bones for so long, began to dissipate. Hiding who I was just to (fail to) fit in had become second nature, an instinctive survival mechanism. I had to learn to become myself.

Becoming myself took some time. It wasn't all simple. In that first, heady year, I still harboured a nagging anxiety that all my friends – all these people who demonstrated again and again that they loved me, just as I was – would somehow disappear. I tried to make myself too palatable, tried to hold on to people too tightly. Honestly, I was clingy. Whenever someone accidentally forgot to invite me to something, my mind spiralled into despair. I still didn't have a model for healthy friendships, especially ones between non-disabled and disabled people. The after-effects of the years of bullying I had endured at school ran deep, but so did the cultural silence. Every time I talked about care or access or pain, I could see my friends grasping for the right words, a look of panic hidden behind encouraging, kind smiles. Not knowing what to say went both ways: my friends were dating, having relationships, having sex, and I didn't really know how to talk about any of it or how not to feel left out. They'd all learned to be comfortable discussing this stuff at school, and I worried desperately about sounding naive when I broached a question or voiced my two cents. Things were so much better – inconceivably better than just a few years earlier – but I never quite felt like I could just fit in.

Still, it was at university that I first learned a vital lesson: just how brilliant, sustaining and life-affirming female friendships can be. How much fun and laughter can be had over a pizza and wine. How good and freeing it feels to dance among people who love you. How completely people who were strangers six months ago can have your back.

Some of my very favourite memories involve studying (ish) side by side in the kitchen, or discussing why we were perpetually into unavailable men over hot chocolate and cake, or, more often than not, just going to lectures and events and Tesco. This kind of intimacy, of just slotting our lives together, was so new to me. It filled me with confidence and taught me, slowly, slowly, to like myself and love the life I was building. I admired these women, was pushed to be a better version of myself by them, but more than anything, I adored them.

As a disabled woman, having such deep female friendships meant everything. To have people who wanted to listen, who gave unfailing support even when they couldn't understand, who let me fall apart and put me back together as many times I needed, was invaluable. Non-disabled women may not know exactly what ableism feels like or how it seeps into every crevice of your life, but the wisest among them can guess that it has more than a little in common with sexism. They know what it is to be judged for your body before you speak, or to have to work twice as hard for half the recognition. They understand how it feels to live in a world not built for you. On the basis of these shared understandings, it is possible to build powerful bonds of solidarity. And we did. Almost a decade later, they are holding firm.

When I graduated from university and returned to London, I mourned for the environment that had made me feel so at home. I think, deep down, I honestly believed that I would never make friends again; that only in the finely tuned and artificially accessible environment of Warwick was such a thing possible. Naturally, I was wrong. Soon, work and life had opened up ever-expanding circles of friends, beyond anything I could have imagined when I'd left London three years earlier.

I was forever traipsing into town for a gig or pub quiz or house party, getting changed in the loos at work before heading out, falling exhausted but happy into bed at some small hour in the morning. I began to be less wary of new people, to enjoy meeting friends of friends and strangers in bars without expecting to be rebuffed or rejected. My group of pals became wider and louder and more rambunctious, and I learned to dance wildly in the centre of a tumble of humans I adored, self-consciousness abandoned at the door.

These friends were incredibly patient as I attempted to work out what being a disabled woman meant in this new, terrifying stage of life apparently called 'adulthood'. It was all quite confusing, but we worked it out together. We deliberated together on whether it was worth struggling our way into an inaccessible venue or to just have fun in the flat. They stood up for me, giving ableists a piece of their minds in ways I found hilarious, impressive and occasionally scary. We chatted about the many failures of feminism in relation to disabled women, but also all women who do not fit the mould. We found our own forms of body positivity and self-acceptance. I began to express what I needed and, eventually, how I was feeling about all this ableism we kept encountering. They learned to recognise when to let me fight my own battles and I learned that it was OK to ask for help emotionally as well as physically. I truly believe that figuring all this stuff out together made the friendships of my early twenties some of the most honest and open of my life. Things in the big wide real world were intense and new and mildly terrifying, but nonetheless we navigated it together, all washed down with many pints of cider and gallons of fun.

To my confusion, though, as time wore on, a nagging sense of loneliness would sometimes rear its head. I would spend the day happy and busy, and then, as soon as I settled down in front of the TV, I would feel overwhelmed with an inexplicable mix of grief and panic. For the first time since school, I felt fundamentally different from the people I knew, always the odd one out, even though, this time, no one treated me that way. That old familiar feeling that I was interacting with life through a frosted glass window returned, as if I was part of and yet simultaneously distinct from the people around me. There was a gulf opening up again that, despite long, emotionally open chats with those I loved, I couldn't seem to bridge. I felt like I was drifting further away. For a while, I couldn't really understand where this feeling was coming from. I was happy, wasn't I? My friends and I loved each other, didn't we? We were having fun, weren't we? It seemed absurd that I could be surrounded by the easy friendships that I had always longed for and yet sometimes feel so alone. I chastised myself for not being able to just enjoy the good times and endeavoured to suppress the bubbling uncertainty that rose in my chest whenever I stopped for a minute. I wondered if my school years had conditioned me to always feel alone even when I wasn't, but I also knew that I hadn't felt like this at university. Why was I haunted by this feeling of detachment? I wondered if it was all in my head.

With half a decade of hindsight (has it really been so long?), I can see clearly what I couldn't see then. I wasn't weird, or bad at friendship, nor did my friends secretly hate me. But nor was I imagining the problem. The gulf I sometimes felt between myself and my friends *was* widening, because our lives were progressively becoming more different again. The truth is, the older (and the further away from Warwick) I got, the more disability and ableism shaped my life and made it different from theirs.

At first, the widening of the gap was almost imperceptible; my worries about care or access (the latter, in particular, suddenly so much worse than it had been at uni) didn't chime with their anxieties about careers or housemates. Then the widening accelerated. Conversations bounced between their decisions to move in with long-term partners to my loneliness in my flat-for-one; from their engagements to my inability to find a date. Don't get me wrong, we didn't stop wanting to hear about each other's experiences, support each other, or share things, it was just that we couldn't relate like we used to. I felt guilty and, occasionally, angry that we didn't seem to understand each other, but eventually, I realised that it wasn't my fault or theirs. If society had been more equal, if it had treated me as I should have been treated, I can guarantee that the gulf would never have loomed so large. It wasn't that we were failing each other, but that ableism was failing all of us.

Comparison is the thief of joy, and yet we all fall into the trap of comparing ourselves to the people around us, especially, as women, to those who are closest to us. In a way, I think it was a sign of how much I adored and valued my friends that our differences bothered me so much. I wanted to be like them because I loved them, and it was the knowledge that I could have been like them if only society was less ableist that prompted those feelings of grief. And the worst thing was, I didn't know how to talk to them about it. I didn't want them to feel guilty, for one thing, but I also literally didn't have a language for these feelings. Just like all those years ago at school, there were no cultural reference points to point to, no larger narratives to hold on to. Everything we are told about female friendship shows navigating life's stages together as the ultimate bonding ritual. We are taught to expect a kind of intimacy that comes from never having to explain, built on giggly gasps of 'Me too!' and 'Oh my God, same!' in response to our hushed but free confessions. Yet I was constantly explaining, always met by empathy but not similarity. I searched and searched for the words that would unlock that communal experience, and I could see in their eyes that they were doing the same. But, despite my love of words, I couldn't find a way to translate a lifetime of ableism into the language of those who had never faced it. For disabled women, then, being locked out of these traditional life stages not only causes direct pain, but also the indirect pain of feeling left out or, worse, left behind. Sometimes, when everyone chatted around me, I had a feeling of being the kid at the adults' table, my life still much the same as it had been at twenty-two, while everyone else's moved on and forward. It made my chest tight, as if I couldn't breathe. I wish there had been a model for what these friendships could look like, one where differences were acknowledged rather than papered over, one where we could meet each other where we were, and one that didn't make me feel like a failure.

I realise that I have written this last paragraph in the past tense – perhaps as a way to distance myself from all these tricky emotions. But in reality, this feeling of drifting away, or perhaps drifting backwards is, I confess, something that I still struggle with. After all, there is an inherent human desire to be understood, to be known, by the people we share our lives with. But I can also recognise that my longing to fit in is a product of deep sexist and ableist social conditioning. There is no real reason for the belief that our friends must understand us in order to love us. Indeed, this just isn't true. Our friends can love us and we can love them even when – sometimes especially when – we have completely different experiences. Differences make our lives richer. Women should not all be the same, and fitting in should not require us to smooth ourselves into more palatable versions of the people we really are. Fitting in can be so much more than being the same or going along the same path. It can be a fit of giggles. A meal shared. A book borrowed. It can be a phone call just to say hello, a link to an esoteric meme, a knowing look at a party. It can be a bad duet to a favourite song, a squeeze of the shoulder, a dormant group chat bursting to life to celebrate good news. It can be a card in the post to make you smile, and sitting outside in a Covid winter just to see each other safely. Most importantly, it can be recognising and acknowledging and celebrating our differences, rather than ignoring them; as my wonderful friends do every time they book an accessible restaurant or come over to secretly vet a new PA. Sometimes, friendship with non-disabled friends can be difficult and painful, but most of the time it is as happy and easy and fun as it would be if ableism didn't so much as exist. I will be eternally grateful for that.

As – often – the only disabled person in the room, I think I will always feel a little bit like an outsider. I can't share in much of my friends' lives, and they can't possibly know, viscerally, the weight of a lifetime of ableism. Such differences will always mean that we cannot replicate the ideals of female friendships we have been spoon-fed since we were little. For me, the legacy of bullying remains etched into my skin, so I only know how to understand myself as the odd one out. No matter the distance I put between myself and school, or how radically things have changed, I will always be on edge about the ways that I do not fit in. It is hard to be different. But that does not preclude great friendships, full of trust and fun and muddling through. It does not preclude complete, wholehearted acceptance or meeting each other exactly where we are. I love my brilliant, hilarious, kind, wise friends. I have no doubt that the reverse is true. For a girl who once felt completely alone, that is victory – happiness – indeed.

Chapter 5

Creating community: Finding my place

If belonging is complicated among my non-disabled friends, I have been extremely lucky to find it in spades among my fellow disabled pals. With hindsight, of course, this is an obvious fact; we can find belonging with people who share our experiences. And yet, it took me quite some time to find it.

As a kid, I didn't notice the lack of disabled people in my life. It was, after all, the only thing I'd ever known, and I didn't think to question it. Still, it was having a subconscious effect. Despite rationally knowing that it couldn't possibly be true, deep down I really believed that I was the only person whose life looked like mine, and that belief made me both scared of the future and determined to ignore the realities of disabled life. As I got older and began to see how people reacted to me – the casual patronising, the refusal to understand my voice, the constant reminders that I was seen as different and less-than – I began to conceive of myself as the outsider, a sore thumb in the crowd. I felt like a puzzle piece that had been tidied away into the wrong box; the picture could be completed without a place or even the need for me. It's one thing for other people to think that you don't belong in the world, and quite another to believe it yourself.

For a long time, I wished for camouflage. All I wanted was to blend in and disappear, and I envied my peers' chameleon-like abilities to follow the latest trend. I longed to go unnoticed. So I made myself quiet, speaking only when spoken to, and perched on the edges of conversations – not quite in and not quite out; hovering in a grey, silent zone. It was far easier to have conversations with people where I was supposed to be different – with teachers or the lovely school caretakers – than with those who reminded me just how much I didn't fit in. When I did try to participate, I was hyper-aware of my voice impediment and my wobbly body, and I would become so tense that I could barely speak. I wanted to talk but I didn't really want to be heard.

I couldn't imagine not being lonely. Indeed, loneliness became a key part of who I was. I was desperate for someone who I could speak to about what was happening to me – the care issues, the bullying, a loss of physical ability as I grew – who would perhaps have experienced something similar. I longed to be understood; heard; known. And I longed for role models – people to look up to, who could reassure me that things would be OK, and who could show me what a good, valuable, happy disabled life could look like. All I wanted was to see someone a little like me. But, despite an agonising search, I could never find them.

Looking back, it boggles my mind that this could be so. Other disabled teenagers were out there, siloed in other schools, and looking for me as desperately as I was looking for them. And disabled adults were out there, too, working and going to the pub and living fulfilling lives. Hundreds, even thousands of people shared my struggles and fears and hopes, they just didn't go to school with me or belong to my family or work with my parents. And, perhaps less accidentally, they didn't appear in any of the TV, newspapers, books or online media I consumed either. They were invisible. Which meant that, to me, they effectively didn't exist.

Until, one day, in the unlikely setting of a fancy health club in West London, they did. It was a stroke of serendipity; my mum had asked my physio if she knew anyone we could talk to about the logistics involved in going to uni, and it turned out that she did – another of her clients had just graduated. My parents and I went off to meet Alex and his parents, and the rest, as they say, is history. As the adults chatted about care costs and accessible accommodation, Alex and I quietly – and fairly awkwardly – got to know each other. A hazy memory sticks in my mind: I was telling some anecdote of being left at the top of the stairs at school, and how frustrating it was, and Alex interjected with an enthusiastic 'I know!' I looked at him in disbelief. No one had ever *known* before. I was sixteen years old.

Alex and I went on to become extremely close friends. I could, and have, talked to him about everything and anything (sorry, Al). In those early years, he helped me to navigate the extremely fraught business of picking a university, leaving home, and having care for the first time. It's important to understand that we weren't mates because we both had cerebral palsy – how weird would that be? – but because we had lots of other things in common, not least a love of writing and a die-hard commitment to be as sarcastic as possible at all times. But the deep, easy understanding of each other's lives did make our friendship stronger and more open, and provided me with my first-ever sense that there were spaces in which I belonged. It is a surprise to precisely no one that we are still friends over a decade later, despite having worked quite literally opposite each other for a few years at the BBC (don't ask)!

Knowing Alex helped me to stop feeling like a freakish anomaly. Things that happened to me also happened to him. When we talked, I didn't have to explain myself or pretend that I was a completely different person. He may have judged me for being an absolute nerd with terrible music taste (he wasn't wrong), but I wasn't being judged for my speech or my care needs or the frustration and fear I felt. This was a revelation, and slowly my self-perception began to change. No longer feeling so alone made it easier to take up space and raise my voice. I began to try new things. I wrote more. I even started talking about disability (it is, frankly, much harder to hate your own disability if you don't hate your best mate's). And, beyond disability, it was just so nice to have a real friend – someone who was kind and met me for coffee and generally treated me in the exact opposite fashion to the Mean Girls at school. Things were looking up. I was on my way.

And then I made it to Warwick, and on the very first day, I found myself sharing a flat with another wheelchair user. By the end of the week, our Flat 19 had teamed up with Flat 3, where another wheelchair-using friend lived with his carers. Pre-drinking in the kitchen involved some pretty fun logistics to get us all round the table, but my body hummed with an easy contentment. Suddenly, I was in a world where PAs, wheelchair maintenance and managing accessibility were just run-of-the-mill. It actually took time to adjust to not having to hide things or smooth them over, to not apologise when we couldn't go to an inaccessible club or when I needed a hand. In my flat, I could ask for whatever it was that would make my life easier, from someone picking something up from the shop to hanging out in my room so I could be comfortable in bed. I disposed of the idea that my needs were an inconvenience or that some realities of disability – needing help changing a sanitary pad, or the dribble that happens because I don't automatically swallow – were too taboo and gross to ever mention. We talked about everything, and as we did, all this shame I had been carrying around began to roll off my shoulders.

How different would my teenage years have been if I'd had a space in which to be myself? Shame isn't a natural response to being disabled. But it is a natural response to being judged and ostracised. It is a natural response to never seeing yourself represented. And it is a natural response to the discomfort, awkwardness and fear which meet any mention of our needs, experiences or bodies. Once I was in an environment in which I was permitted to just be myself, I found it remarkably easy to do so. And without shame, other seemingly impossible developments followed easily.

I stopped hating my voice and so lost my fear of public speaking. I stopped hating my body, and therefore began to dress however I liked. My natural but long-buried tendency towards activism began to emerge once more; partly because I was empowered by advocating for the people I loved, but also because I now felt that I deserved better. Eventually, I stopped thinking of my disability as a flaw and instead as just a neutral part of who I was, as unworthy of judgement as my blue eyes or blonde hair. I was beginning to find confidence in my identity. My disabled friends – Alex and Anna and Kurt and so many others – created a world in which I was finally happy to be who I was.

After the wrench of leaving my little Warwick idyll, I was incredibly fortunate to be hired by the BBC through its Extend in News scheme, which was designed to get more disabled journalists to work for the broadcaster. Not only was this a phenomenal career opportunity, but it meant I started my working life with a big group of friends with whom to navigate workplace ableism, plot career moves and, most importantly, go to the pub on a Friday. It made the whole 'being a twenty-two-year-old disabled woman working for a major broadcaster' thing much less terrifying than it otherwise would have been (it was still pretty terrifying).

One of the most reassuring things was being able to check that you weren't 'imagining it' – whether 'it' was a colleague who couldn't look you in the eye, or an editor's refusal to use better language when covering disability. The Extend WhatsApp group chat was a source of solidarity and understanding in an organisation where disabled voices could be undervalued and overlooked. It was also the source of much hilarity (disabled people have the best banter) and, over time, some of my firmest friendships. (Paul and Nalina, what would I do without you?) My time at the BBC was a bit of a rollercoaster when it comes to disabled-woman stuff, but I am very grateful to Auntie Beeb for expanding my circle of disabled friends into a small but raucous tribe.

As brilliant as they can be, though, a group of disabled friends can only do so much for you. They can commiserate when your chair breaks down. They can understand why a crap carer is stressing you out. They can raise an arched eyebrow when a stranger patronises you and laugh when the sight of two disabled people out in the world together causes abject panic. But they can't give you a sense of your place in the wider world. They can't teach you about the social model until it sits deep in your bones, and they can't help you learn the line between useful advocacy and banging your head against a wall. They can't open up disability history and, being a generally similar age to you, they can't act as role models. And because there are only so many disabled people at your school or uni or workplace who you have anything in common with, you can't create disabled-majority spaces together to act as a salve when an abled world leaves you raw and smarting.

For all of this, what's needed is a wide-angle lens; not a friendship group, but a community. Growing up, I didn't even know such a thing was possible, let alone how big, diverse, supportive and friendly it would turn out to be. I started out small, following a few disabled writers and activists on Twitter amongst a torrent of political pundits (all of whom, by the way, were not disabled). Every now and then, I would scroll past a tweet that reflected an experience I'd had but never heard articulated by someone else before. I'd feel a flash of recognition. The few activists I knew would retweet others they knew into my feed, and I'd follow them too. Slowly, my Twitter account transformed from a stream of repeated political rumour to a diverse, informative collection of different experiences and perspectives. I started to properly learn about what it's like to live with different impairments, and the subtle differentiation in the ableism faced by, say, autistic people, blind people and wheelchair users. I could see how all these little things added up to systemic patterns of exclusion, silencing and othering. Over and over again, I was reassured that no, I wasn't imagining it. All the unremarked-upon moments of ableism that had shaped my life began to coalesce, and for the first time ever, I understood myself as a disabled person – as one of these people who made up a community defined by mutual aid, solidarity and a great deal of gallows humour.

In my mind's eye, a web of support spread out, IP address linked to IP address, smartphone linked to smartphone, pulling more and more people into something new, something radical: a community where each and every one of us belonged.

Still, over time I noticed a pattern on 'disability Twitter' – the experiences I heard about were overwhelmingly . . . male. It wasn't that all the tweeters were men – far from it – but that what we talked about was generalised to supposedly all disabled people, and ignored the specific realities of existing as a disabled woman. I saw hundreds of tweets about the inaccessibility of public transport, but almost none about, say, dating as a disabled woman. Access was talked about as it pertained to strong men in manual wheelchairs, but few people ever raised the issue of sanitary bins in disabled loos. The trend was matched in my own friendships. I had what I'd always dreamed of – two disabled best friends, Alex, and then Paul, who I called when things were funny or bizarre or just a bit scary; who were – are – my ride or dies – and yet there remained things I couldn't speak to them about. Because, as I never let them forget, they are boys. And while they are truly the best of friends – empathetic, hilarious and somehow never tired of my chronic need for reassurance – there are some experiences so specific to being a very visibly disabled woman that they cannot understand or offer advice on, much as they would like to. Having Alex and Paul in my life these past few years has made many things much easier to deal with and – the greatest gift of all – made loneliness a thing of the past. My Twitter community did the same, giving me somewhere to vent and find answers, to express and receive solidarity, and to see myself as part of something bigger. But I still longed, just as I had as a teenager, to see myself and my intertwining identities fully represented. And I still longed for role models.

When Covid hit, I unsurprisingly had a lot of free time – and for once in my life I wanted a break from the news. Twitter was thus a no-go zone outside working hours, but I needed something else to mindlessly scroll. I turned to Instagram. And to my surprise, I found a whole load of – you guessed it – disabled women! Not just any disabled women: disabled women who were powerchair users, disabled women with PAs, disabled women with jobs, disabled women who were activists, disabled women in fashion, disabled women with kids. That is, disabled women who had lives that either resembled mine or, even better, looked like what I hoped mine could one day. They'd been out there all along. And, fabulously, they were sharing how they did it all – the challenges and the successes, the frustrations and the joys – in ways that reflected my own complicated relationship with disabled female life. Those pandemic months were dark, scary days to be a disabled person – more isolated than ever before, we saw the value of our lives cheapened to justify lifting the measures keeping us safe – but through my screen, I found solace and understanding. Slowly, as I commented and reacted to stories and started to post about my own experiences, I began to make real friends. There were Jennie and Gem from Sociability – an app giving disabled people access information – and Sophie M off the telly. Rebekah and another Sophie, who shared their experiences of disabled motherhood. Fellow journalists Lydia and Rachel and Chloe, writing about all the things that people wanted hidden away. All of these disabled women were experiencing and sharing the curious mix of ableism and sexism that I was forever struggling to articulate. Seeing my reality, in all its complexity, reflected back to me for the first time was electrifying, empowering and invigorating. Indeed, the confirmation that what I was experiencing was happening to other people is one of the things that led me to embrace activism and write this very book.

My community was growing, but during Covid it was still divided between an offline and online world. I longed to meet some of the fabulous disabled women I was talking to on Instagram in real life and feel that warm glow of connection. I couldn't see a way of making it happen; even without the threat of a global pandemic, we all lived so far apart, had busy lives, and in some cases had incompatible care hours. But then, just as the world started to open up, the perfect opportunity presented itself. I was asked by the *Guardian* to review *Then Barbara Met Alan*, the first-ever mainstream drama about the disability rights movement, which meant – humblebrag – I got to go to the preview screening at the BBC.

What a thing to experience. A room full – full! – of the great and the good of disability culture and politics. I could scarcely believe that it was real. For the first time in my life, I was in a space where more people were (visibly) disabled than not. I met and chatted to so many people I admired; people doing cool, interesting, important work on behalf of the millions who weren't there. I even spoke to Barbara Lisicki – the real-life heroine of the show – who was the pioneering activist behind the successful campaign for the DDA, Britain's first law protecting disabled people from discrimination. The evening was inspiring, but mostly it was a hell of a lot of fun.

Disabled people are not, of course, all best friends as soon as we meet – sorry to disappoint the stereotypists – but there is a level of camaraderie that makes getting to know each other easy and relaxed in a way it can never be when you're navigating non-disabled spaces. What I really noticed, too, was the extra bond that comes when talking to disabled women; the particular way we can, with a certain and deliberate choice of words, make each other feel confident in our appearance and needs. For the first time I could remember, I was in public and didn't feel awkward about being a little messy when I ate. I didn't feel the need to attempt to communicate a request to my PA solely using my eyebrows. A lightness flowed through me. It was one of the times in life where I have been most happy to be myself.

At the end of the night, I got into a taxi and cried big, dollopy tears. My adult self had had a wonderful time, but I wasn't crying for her. I was crying for the little girl, for the teenager, who had spent all those years looking for somewhere to belong. I was crying for those years of loneliness and fear. But I wasn't crying because I was sad. I was crying because I was so happy; happy to have survived it all, happy to be living a life I could not possibly have imagined. Happy, most of all, to know that there were spaces out there for me, where I could breathe easily, laugh easily, exist easily. I had made it to the end, in many ways; to the end of the road I first started down when I met Alex a decade before. I had a life and friends and a community to love. I didn't have to keep looking for the next level of acceptance; I'd reached them all. I could rest here for a while.

What's funny is that, in the few short months since the BBC event, I have found myself in disabled-majority spaces again and again. Each time, I come away with the same relaxed, energised buzz; high on my own good fortune. I am incredibly lucky to move in circles of brilliant disabled people. The same can be said for the serendipity involved in making connections online – the random algorithm-generated suggestions leading to solid friendships. But every time I am struck by the novelty of these spaces, on and offline, I wonder how it can possibly be that I have only just found them. How can I have waited so long? All the disabled people I meet at the moment are my age or older. By definition, then, they have been around for my entire life. Often, when celebrating the power and brilliance of our community together, we have to pause and ponder: where have we all been hiding?

The truth, of course, is that we hadn't been hiding. The world had hidden us. Literally, in the sense that inaccessibility keeps so many disabled people inside and out of view, so that of course we can't find each other. But we have also been hidden in a deeper sense, too – kept off the telly and out of magazines and newspapers because our opinions, experiences and perspectives have never been deemed valuable. Our voices have never been listened to. Our experiences have always been seen as niche, irrelevant to the mainstream society we are not thought to belong to. Our stories go untold; we have been silenced. And you simply can't find community if you can't (metaphorically) hear or see the people who make it up.

This is even more true when it comes to my search for disabled women. For us, that casual lack of representation turned into a gaping void. The routine erasure of our existence in popular culture, particularly elements of that culture aimed at women, contributed to my feeling that disability and womanhood couldn't co-exist, and that no one else was experiencing the complex intersection of these identities the way I was. It kept me apart from other disabled women, because, for a long time, I didn't even realise I should be looking for them, let alone understand where I might start. To put it another way, until recently the lack of representation for disabled women actively prevented us from forming any sort of community at all.

The media landscape hasn't really changed all that much in terms of disability representation (trust me, as a disabled journalist covering disability, I am acutely aware of what is and isn't deemed worth printing). But social media has empowered disabled women to reach beyond and around traditional gatekeepers. We no longer have to convince commissioning editors that our stories are worth telling; we simply tell them ourselves. Each Instagram post about disabled fashion, disabled dating, disabled motherhood, is a marker, a stake in the ground to say we are here. We exist. And each comment and share and message holds up a big banner to say, *me too, you are not alone, here is where you belong*. From there, it is suddenly much easier to say, 'Let's go for a drink,' and find yourself not only seeing disabled women through your screen but right there in front of you, nursing a pint, cursing the world and laughing. Laughing because you are together at last, against the odds, and how glorious it is to be here.

All of which means that, finally, remarkably, not only do I have disabled friends and a disabled community, but also the one last thing I was still looking for: role models. Disabled women to look up to, to admire, to follow in their wheel-tracks. Navigating life without a visible outline for how it might go has always been pretty scary. I've never known what was possible and what was not until I went out and tried it. There was never anyone to ask for advice or about how they did something; never anyone who could listen to my fears about the future and tell me it would be OK (well, not anyone I believed, anyway). I had to tell myself it was doable, and then I had to work out how to do it. Mostly, what I spent all those years wanting was a disabled woman who could model a good, disabled, female life to me. I wanted to know I could be successful; that such a thing was possible for me. I wanted to know I could have fun; that things wouldn't always be so hard. I wanted – desperately – to know I could be happy. It is so hard to be what you can't see, but I had to find my own way along the unlit path. I was beginning, before these women finally found me, to take bolder strides into the gloom of the future. But how wonderful it is that just as I pushed forward, they took my hand and helped me switch on the streetlamps ahead.

Here is what I now know to be true, thanks to these women: a good, disabled, female life is out there for the taking. Reaching out towards it may be gruelling work at times, but it is possible. And while that good life may not sync with the good lives you see around you or in the movies, it is no less worthy of celebration. You are no less worthy of getting what you want and doing what you love. Your disabled hopes and dreams and fears and doubts are as valid as the more traditional ones you're more used to seeing being honoured and accepted. There are many ways to live well. There are many ways to be happy. Go out and get it – people are here to help.

Finding a place among my disabled friends and then the wider community changed my life immeasurably for the better. I have learned so much, made so many good memories, and become infinitely more confident, at ease with myself, and proud to be who I am. These days, more often than not, I am happy. All of this makes it even more of a shame that the value of this community and its people – their wit and strength and generosity – is still so overlooked by non-disabled society. If only people would see that there is so much good here, they could learn from us all the things that I have learned: the strength of community, the power of activism, and just how proud to be disabled it is possible to be.

I cannot imagine, now, how I spent sixteen whole years without knowing a single disabled person. The way this absence shaped my conception of myself still lingers into adulthood. But how life has changed since then. From meeting Alex for the first time, to being one of many disabled students at Warwick; from the support of my Extend crew at the BBC to being part of a huge online community, each step on the way has reassured me, comforted me and given me confidence. Life is so much less scary now, with role models to look up to, and it is so much less lonely, too, with good friends around always, whether in the phone in my hand, or sitting around my kitchen table. These are the friends who make me feel known, loved, accepted; with whom I never feel ashamed or different or left behind. They have taught me so many things. Most importantly, they have taught me where it is that I truly belong. I am so proud that it is amongst this glorious crowd of people I adore.

Chapter 6

Dating: Locked out of love

The email from the dating agency read: 'We have never had success with a wheelchair user. We advise you not to become a member until we have set up a specific site for the disabled.' I read it sitting on my bed, getting dressed, with my then-PA, Laura. I remember my heart starting to beat faster and my vision narrowing as the adrenaline kicked in. I remember wanting to say something but not being able to breathe. I remember silently handing Laura my phone so she could read it for herself.

Oddly, it was seeing her digest what I'd just read that started the tears. And in that old cliché, once I'd started, I couldn't stop. A stunned Laura sat down beside me and just let me cry, her hand working its way into my balled fist. She didn't know what to say. Unusually, neither did I.

I'm not sure how long we sat there, but at some point I decided to call Alex. I wanted someone who would understand. I wanted someone I could sob to. He was at work and in a meeting, but the unusualness of a mid-morning phone call was enough to elicit a panicked text. 'What's up?' I screenshot the email and texted it to him, no accompanying comment necessary. While he worked out what to say, I managed to get dressed and go to the loo.

There's a second half to this story, one not quite of redemption but definitely of reclamation. But before I tell it, let me first tell you how I found myself here, being slapped in the face by an email.

The story really starts, as all the stories in this book seem to do, in my teenage years. Of course, I was pretty used to being left out by then. And yet, I still noticed when the girls around me started dating the boys from the boys' school, and I did not.

Somewhere around this time, it pains me to say, I made the mistake of googling 'disability and relationships'. This, I cannot stress enough, was a terrible idea. Not only did I find some frankly terrifying stuff about fetishists, but I also stumbled across some statistics apparently showing how few disabled people were in relationships.[1] I didn't yet know that most statistics are unreliable, and instead took this to be gospel truth. I started to wonder if being disabled meant being alone romantically as well as platonically, and all the available evidence suggested that it did. The future felt even bleaker. A sense of panic set in, and it didn't leave for another decade. I shut the laptop, and didn't tell another soul what I'd read for five long years.

Despite what I'd read, I reassured myself that I was still at school, and not only were the available boys really not my type, but also I didn't do any of the activities – drama, music or, God forbid, sport – where my classmates in our all-girls school were meeting the boys from the accompanying boys' school. I thought I had time. I thought things would change once I had escaped the claustrophobic world of education. And, I told myself over and over again whenever that Google session crossed my mind, no other statistic had ever held me back. Surely I could ignore this one too.

University, I thought, was my chance. Many of my brilliant new friends were single too, and we were able to chat and giggle and bemoan the men we fancied. We could dare each other to ask for someone's number (we never did) and go through each other's Tinder options and swipe right on deeply unsuitable men, laughing at the ensuing bizarre chats. Briefly, fleetingly, I felt like I was moving at the same speed as the people I loved.

---

1 Of course, I cannot now find these stats – although a qualitative report from Baylor College of Medicine found that 58 per cent of disabled women surveyed were single, compared to 45 per cent of non-disabled women, and that those with particular kinds of impairments (including cerebral palsy) or who acquired their impairment early in life were more likely to have negative dating experiences.

And then all of a sudden I wasn't. Silly dating turned into proper relationships. People didn't want to go clubbing so much as they wanted to stay in and watch a film with their new partners. My friends were really good at making sure I never felt like the third wheel, and they protected our time together too. But as they paired up, I once again began to wonder what life held for me. The feeling of being left behind crept in once more.

My friends, I think, wanted to believe that my disability had nothing to do with it. To be fair to them, I was, at the time, painfully shy, and even more painfully in love with someone who shall remain nameless. My friends reckoned that I wasn't putting myself out there. They didn't see the men who unmatched with me on Tinder when they realised I couldn't walk, or the ones who turned away in disgust when I said hello at the bar. They didn't see that no one ever looked at me as a potential date, or the fact that I was always called pretty rather than attractive. They didn't see that the man who kissed me once in the student club in Coventry then went back to high-five his mates. I told the story as a joke for years, but actually I knew he'd kissed me on a dare. Every time someone told me to just put myself out there, I wanted to scream: 'Don't you see what happens when I try?'

They also didn't know about those statistics that had wormed their way into my psyche. They made it hard to believe that putting myself out there was worth it. But I did try, over and over again, downloading each new app, forcing myself to adopt a pained hopefulness despite the fact that they made me miserable every single time, and starting conversations in pubs that left me feeling sick. I left university still single.

Nevertheless, as they say, I persisted. I went back to London and re-downloaded the apps yet again. I asked out a few acquaintances, a process that never ended well. I even, finally, eventually, and much too late, asked out the person I'd loved for so long. I'd say it didn't go to plan, except that I had always planned for it to go badly – and it did.

The heartbreak temporarily floored me. Life was going well – I had a good job and excellent friends who I adored – but I was fixated on the emptiness in the flat, by the space beside me on the sofa on Saturday nights spent with the TV. And as my friends' relationships got more serious, the panic mixed with something I hadn't felt since school: not really loneliness but aloneness. Every time someone moved in with a partner, bought a flat or got engaged, I felt guilty for wishing that they could just wait a little longer; give me time to catch up. But their lives kept moving forwards, and I was always sitting still.

Just before the pandemic, I had two dates through Hinge, the new app on the block. I was twenty-five, and these were the first dates of my life. One was comically bad, as I had somehow managed to find a man who didn't like anything: he didn't like travel, the theatre, his job, or seemingly even his own friends. Confession: over the course of a single glass of wine, I began to feel much better about myself. Second confession: when he messaged me the next day to say he didn't think that it would work out between us, I couldn't even be bothered to reply.

The other date went surprisingly well. I'd been really nervous, because we'd been messaging a lot, and I already kind of liked him. We'd even talked about my carers and he'd been remarkably unfazed when I had to rearrange our first meeting because one of them was sick. I thought, with a heady mix of hope and trepidation, that I might have found what I'd been looking for. The date was lovely, too. I'd suggested we meet at the Tate, because I figured that looking at something would take the pressure off looking at each other, but the art was really obscure, and we realised we'd actually quite like to chat, so before long we ended up at the pub. You might know the one, on the river by the Tate, with the most spectacular view of London. As we sat there, each with a pint, laughing and getting to know each other, looking out at my favourite skyline, I wondered if I just might be on the brink of something new and exciting.

The conversation carried on for the rest of the week, and we mentioned meeting up again, but when it came down to setting a date to do so, he decided that we lived too far apart. We stopped messaging. I choose to believe him that the distance was the problem, because he gave me no reason not to take him at his word, and yet in the small hours, I can't help but wonder if maybe my life was just a bit too much for this nice, quiet man.

You might be wondering how I went from starting to date to receiving that dating agency email. The short answer is that the pandemic happened. The long answer is that those two dates were the only ones to come out of dozens of horrid Hinge conversations. In the hazy half-life of the break between the first and second lockdowns, I tried to start dating again. But something had happened in the hollow space of isolation, and I was met by an onslaught of hostility. I was used to mentions of my disability being met by ghosting, but I was surprised by the nastiness of the comments I received, often angrily telling me how I was wasting their time. One guy was very chatty, and professed to be OK about the whole situation until he randomly asked me if I had a speech impediment. *Yes*, I replied, *but everyone understands me*. He told me not to worry – I wondered why he felt the need to reassure me – but after a few more messages, the conversation ended. I figured I had nothing to lose, and asked what had happened. He claimed that he'd decided to concentrate on his music instead of dating. This one, I couldn't convince myself to believe, even if I wanted to.

We'd been talking for a while, and the knowledge that someone who seemed perfectly pleasant had decided I was undateable because of my voice hit hard. I realised that waiting to see if a succession of men I didn't even know would judge a disability they didn't even understand was driving me slowly mad. I went around feeling queasy, anticipating another awful message. *I can't keep doing this*, I thought, *I'm going to delete the apps and enlist some help.*

The idea of using a dating agency made me feel both anxious and fairly embarrassed. I had a nagging sense that it was a terrible idea. So, I canvassed my friends for their opinions. I knew that my friends Becky, Becky and Rachy would all be in favour of the idea, and I was secretly hoping that the more reserved Sophie and Rachel would ask me what on earth I was doing. When each and every one of them told me to go for it – 'What have you got to lose?' – I realised I was now going to have to actually pick up the phone. I told myself that it was worth trying for six months; maybe the experts could help me with what I couldn't do by myself, and if not, at least I'd tried.

On the phone to a lady who seemed really supportive, I mentioned my cerebral palsy. I knew by now that this was going to be crucial information. She thanked me for letting her know, told me not to worry, and asked me to put some details about it on the application form, just so they had all the information.

Before I tell you what happened next – and trust me, it's a humdinger of a story – let's pause here and take a look around. Because while this is an incredibly personal story, it's not one that unfolded in isolation. It is, instead, a crystal-clear reflection of life at the intersection of disability and womanhood – a perfect illustration of how wide and deep the forces of ableism and sexism run in society. Before you can understand what happened to me, you need to understand how it is possible that it happened at all.

There are so many reasons that dating and relationships are among the hardest aspects of life to navigate as a disabled woman – and so many things that could be different. It's not just a case of people being horrible. One of the things those around me struggle the most to understand is that my trouble with dating is not just down to men being actively ableist (although there's a lot of that too); it is rather that society has conditioned these men to see disabled women like me as completely separate from the spheres of dating and relationships. It is not that a man sees me on a dating app and consciously decides that he doesn't want to date a disabled woman, but that he sees me and wonders what the hell I am doing there. The same is true when I meet someone out and about; no man is asking himself if he fancies me, or trying to figure out if I am flirting or just friendly. The question never enters his mind. Disabled women like me are put in a separate box altogether, one completely outside the framework of dating and relationships.

Several factors lie behind this phenomenon, not least the assumption that disabled people are unworthy of love. Just consider the fact, if you will, that Channel 4 happily and proudly calls its popular show about disability and dating *The Undateables* – and then tries to pass it off as an act of anti-ableist allyship. Yikes. Society has so successfully marginalised and othered disabled people that we cannot be seen as potential partners; instead, we are the people that the school football team captain only takes to prom in the hopes of going viral on TikTok. When disabled people – often those seen as more acceptable, more 'normal' – do find love, our partners are either viewed with suspicion (they can't really like us, they must be taking advantage of us) or as saints (how lovely that they chose to have a worse life for us). No one ever considers the brilliant things disabled people bring to relationships or the fact that – I'm sorry to be the one to tell you – the non-disabled person they are in love with could become disabled at any time. There is instead a stifling emptiness where representation should be. There aren't any romcoms with disabled protagonists (except for that one where the guy kills himself at the end to free his girlfriend from the burden of his disability, which is neither 'rom' or 'com' if we're being honest). There aren't any Valentine's Day cards featuring disabled people or listicles about the best accessible dates. There aren't any love songs about the intimacy of care or the stunning disabled girl who lives next door. Disabled people are completely invisible in the never-ending, incessant cultural discussion around dating; is it any wonder the men I encounter don't give me a second thought?

As if this big, stony wall of cultural silence wasn't enough, there are of course our old friends infantilisation and desexualisation to contend with as well. They're obvious from the small startle that passes across a colleague's face when you mention you have a date that evening. They're obvious when your invite to a wedding is tacked on to your parents', while everyone else's come with plus ones. They're obvious in the fact that disabled people having sex is still the ultimate taboo. How can you possibly be seen as a catch or a potential partner if you are still seen as a child?

These problems are common to all disabled people attempting to navigate the peculiar horror of modern dating. But disabled women face specific problems, too. Desexualisation and infantilisation are, unsurprisingly, applied to us in specific and often particularly grim ways. The first, simply put, is the idea that our bodies are not and cannot be seen as attractive.

This is unsurprising, given how many people remain convinced that disabled people's bodies are flawed and broken (the social model hasn't exactly taken the dating scene by storm). Add in the societal pressure on, and assumptions about, women's bodies, and disabled women face a double whammy of exclusion. There is an impossible standard to meet, and disabled women are assumed, without anyone interrogating the thought, to be as far from meeting it as it is possible to be. The fact is that today's dating culture – dominated by split-second decisions to swipe right based on a superficial profile – only encourages the reduction of women's entire lives to a selfie. Show a mobility aid or visible impairment in said selfie and you're doomed to be ignored or, worse, verbally abused. But delay the reveal until you've built up a rapport and risk being subjected to the vitriol that comes when a man finds out he has accidentally fancied – even for a split second – a disabled woman; feeling emasculated, they can lash out in deeply unpleasant ways.

So here's a little secret: disabled women *are* attractive and hot and sexy, and people are often attracted to us (did you think we didn't know?). But the idea is so taboo that people – men and women alike – will perform quite spectacular mental and linguistic gymnastics to pour cold water on any sense of a spark. I think of all the times that I have been called 'pretty', or 'cute', in a slightly patronising or even faintly surprised way, in a bid to put me back into a more comfortable box. It is never 'beautiful' and certainly not 'sexy' (except from my friend Rachy, which is one of the many reasons I love her). I think of all the times I have been called 'pretty for a disabled girl', as if this is somehow a compliment. Do you see the obvious, grim implication, separating disabled women from non-disabled women? And the use of the word 'girl' leaving me stranded in prepubescence and therefore outside the realm of the fanciable? You might not have noticed, but let me assure you that I always do.

For the avoidance of doubt, then, let's clear something up. Disabled adults are adults. Therefore, disabled people have sex. Disabled women have sex. This is, frankly, all I am going to say on the matter, because you should just believe me and, if you don't, Google is your friend. OK? Cool. Moving swiftly on (my parents are reading this . . .).

The other particular issue for disabled women trying to date is the presumption that in any relationship we would be a burden; which is also the source of the grim notion that anyone who went out with us would be, by default, a saint. This load of ableist nonsense seems to be turned up tenfold when we're talking about disabled women in heterosexual relationships, because society is still wedded to old-fashioned and frankly bullshit gender roles. No matter how much progress we think we have made, it all appears to go out the window when disabled women enter the dating world. I honestly couldn't tell you how many times men on dating apps told me they wouldn't go out with me because they didn't want to care for me, which is not only hurtful and inaccurate (I employ a whole team of people to do it, pal), but makes me worried for the day the women they do end up with get the flu or, you know, have a baby. (By the way, my male disabled friends have never been told this by a dating-app stranger.) It goes both ways, too; not only are they horrified that they might have to care for me, but concerned that they wouldn't receive the domestic care society has taught them to expect from women (God forbid they have to do all the cooking). Care is, surely, an essential part of any loving, intimate relationship, and disabled women can of course provide the emotional care that should be present in a partnership, but in our society the expectation remains that physical caregiving should only ever flow one way, from the woman to the man. Honestly, count me out.

Thinking about it now, strict gender roles and assumptions about who can fill them seem to be at the heart of almost all the problems I have faced with dating. There is a reason that, when someone kindly responded to my dating-agency story with a compilation of stories about happy disabled–non-disabled couples, the most noticeable pattern was how few of them were visibly straight. Perhaps being freed from the assumptions about gender that underpin straight relationships allowed these people to free themselves from assumptions about disability too. But so many people are still wholeheartedly wedded to them, and it is disabled women like me who pay the highest price for traditionalism. From the split-second judgements about who is and who isn't attractive, to worries about sex and caregiving, women in straight relationships are assigned roles that disabled women are deemed unable to perform. Of course, the roles themselves are limiting and old-fashioned and crap, but somehow being excluded from even the chance of filling them is still deeply hurtful, because from the moment we are conscious, society has conditioned us to want these stereotypical relationships. It's a funny old world.

Perhaps this complex reality – the pain of being excluded from roles you know to be wrong – is why feminism and the disability rights movement are remarkably silent on this particular issue, despite it being such an important frontier in the fight for equality and inclusion. You would think the crucial part gender roles play in excluding disabled women from dating and relationships would make this a key battleground in the politics of women's liberation, but once again the specific challenges and situations faced by disabled women are left out by our mainstream, homogenised feminism.

This is most obvious in the case of desexualisation; feminism is so focused on freeing non-disabled women from hypersexualisation that those of us at the other end of the scale don't get a look in. If feminism could instead see that both problems come from the same root cause – denial of sexual agency – it could perhaps tackle both, rather than combatting one at the expense of the other.

The same can be said for other issues that affect disabled and non-disabled women in opposing ways; the pressure to prioritise romantic relationships above all else, say, or expectations about the provision of care. If we simply focused on ripping up these false, damaging underlying assumptions, we could liberate all women, disabled and not, from the sexist, ableist structures that dominate the world of dating and relationships. Feminism needs to recognise the power of working for everyone.

So does the disability rights movement. In fairness, there has been a recent recognition of the importance of these issues – a recognition that to be truly equal, disabled people need to be able to date, have sex and form relationships; to be represented in bedrooms as well as boardrooms. Still, I detect some queasiness or reluctance in acknowledging that the issues faced by disabled women are different from those faced by disabled men, perhaps because on this particular topic, we are *all* subjected to a lot of crap. The movement's quite male focus on independence stops it from making the difficult but necessary case for interdependence. I think, too, there is a sense that it is too painful to talk about, or that doing so might elicit too much unwanted pity. It is easier to talk about restricted access to public transport than it is about a lack of intimacy and love. But if the movement should learn anything from feminism, it is that the personal is political: if we are not equal in the search for romance, we are not equal anywhere.

It's a particularly toxic and overlooked combination of ableism and sexism, then, that makes dating as a disabled woman so utterly soul-destroying. The assumptions made about disabled women culminate in the belief that we are undateable and unlovable. This is so obviously false that at times the injustice and unfairness of it all makes me want to scream. But the truth is that no matter how good you are at unpacking the ableism and sexism around you (and I consider myself an expert), being constantly labelled as unattractive, other and unlovable has a profound effect on how you see yourself. It is just so pervasive that despite how hard you try to argue against it, it is difficult, perhaps even impossible, not to internalise some of this misogynistic ableism. As your friends and peers move through dating and relationships with apparent ease, it is difficult not to feel both left behind and as if there is something fundamentally wrong with you. This horrid feeling is only exacerbated by the bizarre, gaslighting refusal of those who love you to acknowledge what is happening; by looking for a less uncomfortable reason for your continued singledom – 'You just haven't found the right guy!', 'You need to put yourself out there!' – they continually shift the blame to you, rather than placing it rightly where it belongs, with ableism.

As I got older, though, I learned enough about the world to know for myself that 'putting myself out there' had absolutely nothing to do with it. OK, maybe I wasn't as out there as I could have been, but I had friends who were shy or quiet and still went on dates and had relationships. It was impossible to ignore what was obviously true, and what it was that made my experiences different from my friends'. But the knowledge that it is misogynist ableism standing in your way doesn't really *change* the fact that it is standing in your way. You might feel marginally better but you don't dismantle oppression simply by knowing it exists. It doesn't go away. And its effects on your life are still incredibly real. The weight of it all can be so crushingly heavy that, in spite of everything you know and all the self-worth you have painstakingly cultivated, in the silence of a sleepless night you *feel* unlovable. Because, after all, you remain unloved.

Of course you internalise that feeling. It's impossible not to. Other issues also fuel the internalised ableism many of us disabled women struggle with when it comes to dating. For me and others I know, the seeds were sown early on, with the abject failure to provide any sort of appropriate, relevant sex education (which happened, one imagines, because absolutely no one thought of us as sexual beings in need of such an education). I can still remember being in Year 9 PSHE, watching those weird animated videos, and thinking *hang on a second, this doesn't look like it's going to work*. When the video finished, we were handed scraps of paper to write questions on and throw into a hat. I looked down at this tiny piece of paper and up at my carer and shrugged. She offered to write something for me, but the room was silent and I didn't want to dictate my question aloud to her. I also didn't want her, a woman double my age who technically worked for my parents, to know what my questions were. And, looking back, I don't think I even believed that the teacher would know how to answer them. I told my carer that I didn't have any questions. No one ever asked me again. And I spent six long years terrified that no one would ever go out with me because maybe I couldn't even have sex.

Thankfully, some friends at university set me straight over a few rum and cokes. But by then, the effect on my sense of self was pretty permanent. It didn't matter that I now knew so much more than I had at the age of thirteen. I had spent my entire teenage life semi-worrying and semi-believing that sex and relationships were for other people, that this whole area of life – and of myself – was off limits. I'd survived that feeling by building a wall between me and the world I thought I couldn't belong in, and despite many years of trying to dismantle it, I have never quite been able to tear it down.

This meant that well into my twenties, I was just a bit awkward about it all. I always felt like a kid playing grown-up. As my friends dated and had relationships, learning things about sex and themselves in the process, I worried that I was too naive and inexperienced. To cope, I denied to myself and to others that I cared, professing over and over again that I just wasn't that interested in sex.

Unsurprisingly, this affected both how I approached dating in general and how I interacted with the particular men I fancied. All the sexist ableism around dating I was exposed to combined with my own internalised feeling that I had absolutely no idea what I was doing, making me nervous and insecure. Despite continually punishing myself on dating apps, in the real world it is hard to deny that I spent a lot of time anxiously avoiding the entire world of dating, relationships and sex. I was almost pathologically averse to the idea that anyone could actually like me, a belief that undoubtedly led to a degree of self-sabotage. I was trapped in a vicious cycle, where self-doubt led to more dating failure and, inevitably, more self-doubt.

How different would things have been if I'd been empowered with relevant information at an earlier age? Here's what I wish they had told me, either at school or in any of the resources I looked for online: that sex is as varied as the people who have it. That disabled people are sexy. That there is no need to be ashamed.

But it's not just sex. I wish they'd told me so many other things about dating and relationships. I wish they had told me that relationships can look like a million different things. That doing things differently is not doing things badly. That there is room for messiness and figuring it out. That I didn't have to be someone's last choice. That there wasn't anything wrong with me. That all of this wasn't my fault. That disabled people are worthy of love.

In fact, the disabled people I know would make some of the very best partners. We already know how to balance competing needs. We are the world's best compromisers. We are empathetic. We see the funny side. But even if we didn't have these particular attributes, we would still be worthy of sex and dating, love and relationships, because everyone is.

The fault, the explanation for why so many disabled people are left out of this vital part of life, lies not with us or with our bodies but with society and how it conceives of relationships. And that's good, because these things can be changed. The ableism and sexism in society are not set in stone. We can imagine something better than this. We can imagine a world where we do not equate disability and unattractiveness, or where men do not abhor the idea of providing care to their partners. We can imagine a world where disabled people are not infantilised and desexualised, and where disabled young people are equipped with the knowledge and confidence they deserve when it comes to sex, dating and relationships. We can imagine a world where disabled women are not so othered that we are shunned and abused. We can imagine a world in which we have stopped measuring disabled women against bullshit gender norms; a world in which we have in fact abolished those very norms. We can – I can – imagine a world in which I am worthy of love.

And yet, despite it all, we must inevitably return to where we started, with that horrible email detonating in my inbox. Because, for all I know about how disabled people deserve and are worthy of love, the truth is that society still doesn't think so. That dating agency certainly didn't. And there is, beyond writing and talking about it, very little I can do to change that.

But this story doesn't end where you perhaps think it does. I don't fall into despair. Nor, obviously, do I find a man. That's not how life works, at least not for me. Instead, I do something a little unusual. I follow someone's advice.

After joining me in outrage and dismay, Alex sends another message: 'At some point you need to share this and write about it.' Even though I now swear that I doubted whether this was such a good idea, the text conversation from the day shows me in complete agreement. Clearly, even in that first moment of deep pain, I recognise that later I will be angry. And Alex knows full well that once I'm angry, I'm incapable of keeping my mouth shut. I text him back: 'I think I might tweet it.'

And of course I do. I can't help myself. I'm still crying as I type, but I feel compelled to show people the attitudes that I know lurk beneath the veneer of acceptance. I press send on my Twitter thread and call Rachy.

By the time I hang up, I have countless Twitter notifications. For a while I just sit and watch the retweets tick up and up and up. Then the messages started coming in, first from people I know and then from complete strangers, tens and then hundreds of comments and direct messages. People tell me I am loved. Disabled people share their own heartbreaking stories of isolation and rejection. But mostly people are shocked, horrified, appalled, and even in my anguish I wonder what it's like to live completely unaware that this is what society is like. Their disbelief annoys me.

The retweets are still going up. My friends are starting to notice. A box of cookies appears at my front door, sent by my big cousin. I wonder what he makes of all this. Ex-colleagues send their thoughts, and my friends call and text and tell me how angry they are. They tell me the agency has it wrong, they tell me I'm a great catch, and I stifle a hundred screams. The agency *isn't* wrong. If people did want to date disabled people, I would never have found myself applying for a dating agency in the first place. That people can't seem to grasp that simple truth makes me even angrier. It feels like a wilful denial of reality. I want to tell them this. I want to ask them how many disabled people they have ever dated. I want to be harsh and bitter. But I don't and I'm not. I know they mean well, that they're trying to help. I also know that they honestly believe what they're saying, which somehow only makes it worse. Anyway, as the day wears on I am simply too exhausted, too broken, too unspeakably sad to argue. I let them comfort me, but I feel no comfort at all.

By now, the tweet has taken on a life of its own. Not an insignificant number of people decide that it'd be worth their time to tell me that the dating agency were just doing me a favour by letting me know that people don't want to date someone like me. As if I didn't already know. As if that helps. But actually the majority of people are kind and angry, and I begin to think that not everyone is terrible. The retweets climb further.

The next morning, the story is covered in *The Times*. I have to call my parents and warn them. Ironically, it's also covered in the *Mail*, the *Sun* and the *Telegraph* (need I say more?). ITV and Sky call – working for the BBC saves me from deciding whether I want to appear on the telly or not. I go on Radio 4, and then realise I should probably have told my editor I was going to do it. She is, thankfully, all for it.

By now, my sadness is beginning to mingle with bemusement. When Becky calls a few days later to tell me they're talking about me on Channel 4's show *The Last Leg*, I simply have to laugh. We have truly entered the realm of the absurd. But there's something else too, a feeling that a conversation has been started that I've never heard before, and that maybe, even if only a little, people have begun to think differently. I've made a crack in the wall of taboo. It's not enough, but it's not nothing either.

Over the next few days, everyone wants to know if I'm OK, but I'm too stunned to know how to begin to answer. Deep down, I know that I am not OK, because I feel as if the top layer of my skin has been peeled off, leaving me raw and exposed. The feeling is surprisingly similar to good old-fashioned heartbreak. I recognise its contours, the initial deep, sharp, winding blow followed by the dull, suffocating ache. All the hope has been sapped out of me. My fighting spirit is completely depleted and, in that moment, I wonder if it'll ever come back. All I want to do is sleep.

And yet. Very quickly but almost imperceptibly, something began to shift. I think it started with the conviction that I never wanted to give a stranger the power to make me this upset again, which prompted the realisation that I'd been allowing exactly that to happen for a third of my life, ever since I'd first downloaded Tinder. Well, no more. I was going to stop allowing people – and life – to repeatedly clobber me around the head.

I asked myself, was all this pain worth the supposed promised land, aka, a boyfriend? The thought repeated, stronger: *all this for a boyfriend? A lousy, hypothetical boyfriend? What on earth have I been doing with my life?*

I haven't opened a dating app since. I turned down another agency who offered to take me on. I no longer enter a pub and scan the room for men to talk to, and have refused friends' offers to set me up with their random colleagues. I am done.

And I am also free. I have stopped defining my life by the

lack of a partner and instead defined it by the presence of friends and so, finally, I am not lonely. I have rejected the rigid, conventional definition of family and instead built one for myself on my own terms; a family made up of friends and PAs, my brilliant parents, and, hopefully one day, children. I have found love elsewhere, where it turned out it has always been. For the first time since my schoolmates started dating those teenage boys, I am not trying to keep up. For the first time since I read those dreadful statistics, I am not trying to prove them wrong. I have laid down my weapons in the perpetual war I have been waging against ableism and sexism, allowed myself to rest, and accepted that I cannot command the tide. I have decided that my real mental health today is more important than deferred, possible happiness tomorrow. I have chosen myself and I have stopped waiting for life to really start. It has started. I am living it. It is completely, thrillingly, goose-bump-raisingly liberating.

This liberation, though, isn't simple. In the years since I stopped trying to find a partner, I have spent an awful lot of energy trying to convince my friends that this was and is the right choice. I maintain that this is true, and that choosing to protect my mental health is not an act of giving up but, actually, the most fundamental way I have ever shown myself love. I am happier and healthier than I have ever been. But having to continually justify this choice to those around me has obscured a messier truth: it is not a choice I ever wanted to make, nor one I made freely. And it is not an easy one to live with.

I feel a profound grief for the life I grew up so desperately wanting and didn't get to live. Every little girl imagines what their grown-up life will look like, and this isn't what mine was supposed to be. I wanted a partner, someone to share in the everyday ups and downs, someone to have dinner with, someone to come home to at the end of the day. I wanted romance, sure, and maybe one day to get married in front of everyone I loved, but more than that I wanted quiet intimacy, to be known and cared for, to not have to face life by myself all the time. I wanted to share a home with someone, to see the world together, and eventually raise some kids in a family that looked like the happy one I grew up in. There is still so much pain and sadness inherent to knowing that a life with that kind of love and commitment is not for me, and anger too in knowing that it is society's sexist ableism that has robbed me of it. I am not *particularly* lonely, but sometimes my flat feels so empty as to be hollow, and I feel the loss of what could have been so acutely that it is physically painful.

The grief is not just for the romantic or love life I wanted, but for the chance I never got to belong in society's narrative of how life should go. From dating as a teenager to first proper relationships at university, from bad date stories to the giggly first throws of romance, from moving in together to getting married, our lives are metered out in a predictable pattern that puts romantic love front and centre. It's how we measure growing up and success; each milestone hit is a sign that we're doing well and moving in the right direction. This might not be right or fair or particularly enlightened, but it is nonetheless a hallmark of the society we live in and the stories we tell about ourselves. The story is so pervasive that being locked out of the narrative feels like being locked out of a real, fulfilling, meaningful life.

I want to pretend that I have no interest in this traditionalist, old-fashioned, sexist narrative, but that's not true. After all, for as long as I have been denied access to it, like every little girl I have spent even longer being sold its value. I can't help but feel deeply sad that none of its promises – companionship, stability, acceptance – will be kept for me. This is one of the few things that doesn't get easier with time and experience.

Maybe the email from the dating agency has lost its caustic sting over the years, but the pain of the gulf between my friends' love lives and mine just grows as that gulf yawns ever wider. I am sincerely happy for them, always, but that happiness is tinged with the sadness of knowing that as their lives move along that narrative, I am still where I have always been. It becomes yet another, incredibly painful, way that I am denied the chance to belong: in a romantic relationship itself, yes, but also in the very pattern of my friends' lives.

On the questions of disability and dating, I don't have any answers – at least not good ones. Whereas I have, in other areas of life, been able to forge my own ways of belonging, when it comes to matters of love, I am as excluded as I have ever been. The forces of ableism and sexism have such a hold over the dating world that I have had, for my own sake, to accept that I cannot simply will them into defeat, or will myself into the relationship I always wanted. That brings, and will always bring, great sadness. That is the truth of it. All I can do, then, is remember not to blame myself, and, looking to a different future than the one I hoped for, to build a life that doesn't centre around this lack of romantic love, that does not define itself by absence. To build new spaces of belonging. To find my own way. It is hard. But I am getting there.

Chapter 7

Motherhood: Looking for hope

I want to be a mum.

It's a simple statement that many women my age make. So many know the deep physical ache of longing; when the sight of a child skipping down the pavement is enough to turn all your racing thoughts to one singular image: a baby in your arms. It's not universal, but so many have quietly wondered what they'd name a girl, or whether they would like one, or two, or even three. What lullabies we'd sing and books we'd read; what colour we'd paint their rooms.

The commonality of this experience amongst my friends should have made this longing something I shared with them, something that made me feel like I belonged in the group. But for many years, the misogynistic ableism that society has piled on to disabled women who contemplate becoming, or indeed do become, mothers has only made me feel further alienated from my peers – and from myself. It has been the source of so much heartache, worry and pain that at times I have simply been unable to speak of it, and at others, been completely overwhelmed by the strength of the forces stacked against me. I have wished for the longing to pass so that I wouldn't have to feel this way any more; have willed it to lift so I didn't live in fear and guilt; have tried desperately to stop caring, so that I didn't have to carry the burden that sexist ableism has heaved upon my shoulders. But the longing for a child has never once lifted, not for a second, and so I have had to carry it around. It is the heaviest thing I know.

I have spent years surrounded by friends' kids, ex-PAs' kids, little cousins. Tiny humans whose hands I have held and heads I have kissed. I know, I am almost sure, every single nursery rhyme. I have pushed swings and read the same bedtime story over and over. And every time I do so, every time I have a baby on my lap, or a toddler under an arm, or just an eye on a child in a park, I feel a sense of calm that I find hard to articulate. I am just in this moment, laughing, delirious with the deliciousness of a giggling child. Is there anything better? I adore them all.

I don't know where it comes from, except that it started, I think, when Stan and Betsy, the now-grown kids of my childhood nanny, were little. These two tiny, gorgeous, incredibly blonde and incredibly kind kids had me head over heels – and whilst they are not so tiny any more, they still do. One under each arm, reading the stories of Paddington Bear, it was these two bundles of cuteness, and the simple, unconditional love we had for each other, who cemented in me the undeniable fact that, one day, I wanted to be a mother.

That realisation, aged maybe thirteen or fourteen, was the beginning of what has now been over a decade of worry. For much of my life, I worried about whether I would be able to look after the child I so desperately wanted. There were so many things I thought I couldn't do with Stan and Betsy: pick them up from the floor, feed them, tie their shoelaces (I couldn't even tie my own). It broke my heart, and convinced me that no matter what I did, I would fail a future child. The idea that I would somehow be a bad mother filled me with a sickly, cloying dread. I could barely speak about it to my friends for fear that they would judge me for wanting to inflict myself on a child. Even with those closest to me, my family and the girls, I found it hard to acknowledge; worried that at some point, someone would tell me that this was something I simply couldn't or shouldn't do. I thought I was wrong to even hope that I could. I was, in all honesty, ashamed that I had the audacity to think about it at all.

My fear that I would be a terrible mother didn't appear out of nowhere; I wasn't just being neurotic. The truth is, everything about how we talk about motherhood – and the things that we don't say – screamed at me that to be a disabled mother would be an abomination; a contradiction in terms. From the myth of the perfect mother – healthy, fit, always present, endlessly capable – to the flawed idea that children should be able to have every single need met by one of two people who must be related to them, every image, advert, plot line told me that I would fail. That my children would suffer in some unspeakable way.

There are a million ways in which disabled women are left out of cultural conversations around motherhood. All the talk is about nappy changing (which I'd need help with), or night feeds (ditto), or doing it all (I already, clearly, do not 'do it all'). If disabled parents are on TV, it is in a news piece about the 'plight' of child carers or, even worse, in a *Children in Need* montage, inevitably accompanied by a Coldplay song. I have, in my life, seen just one positive representation of disabled parenthood in the mainstream media, and that was in a documentary literally called *We Won't Drop the Baby*, in which a disabled couple talk about the negative and prying comments they receive when out with their kids. Even these not-exactly-ideal or reassuring representations of disabled parenting are so few and far between that, for a lot of my life, it simply felt as though disabled mums didn't really exist.

This failure to represent disabled parents has real-world implications. The internet is full of stories of disabled parents being openly challenged when out with their kids. At the supermarket; at school drop-off; even just during a trip to the park – people go out of their way to label disabled parents as selfish, incapable and a danger to our kids. I cannot begin to imagine how much it hurts to have your love for your own child questioned. But I also cannot imagine how it must feel for a child to have that love questioned and, as they get older, to have to defend their parents from an ableism they can't possibly understand. I began to feel guilty for the vicarious ableism any child of mine would have to experience, simply because the world doesn't want me to be their mum.

It's not just cultural issues that made me feel that I was destined to scar my kids for life – services and the law told me the same thing. For a long time, if you googled 'help for disabled parents' or looked for support groups on Facebook, as I often did in the small hours, you would be redirected to services for the non-disabled parents of disabled kids. This has started to change, but only recently. Similar Google searches dredged up web pages with titles such as 'How will having a disabled parent damage my child?' There was no encouragement, no good stories to outweigh the unrelenting misery.

Then there is the really scary stuff. Did you know that, in half of all US states, a child can be taken away from their parent simply because the parent is disabled – without social workers having to prove that the child is suffering in any way? In the UK, disabled parents theoretically have the same rights as non-disabled parents, but routinely have their motivations and fitness questioned by social workers. The message is clear: we should not have kids.

In many ways, the assumptions made about disabled women and motherhood are diametrically opposed to those faced by our non-disabled friends. Non-disabled women are forever being asked when they're going to have kids, with very little consideration of whether or not they actually want them or, indeed, can have them. Both non-disabled women and disabled women face the myth of motherhood as the ultimate ideal, and yet it is foisted upon us in opposing ways. For non-disabled women, the ideal becomes an assumed aspiration: why would you, as a woman, not want to embody it? For disabled women, the ideal is unreachable, an unrealistic expectation held up as proof of our incapability. For all of us, there is anguish. But because the experience is so different, it can be hard for us to understand each other.

For much of my twenties, many of my friends couldn't understand why I was so worried about having kids. It would happen or it wouldn't, they reasoned, just as it would or wouldn't happen for them. Some of them were busy trying to untangle whether they actually wanted kids, or had just been conditioned to think they did, whilst others were just trying to avoid getting pregnant before they could afford it. Either way, a lot of our conversations boiled down to a suggestion – often said between the lines – that I should just chill out about it for a while. I struggled to explain that this was easier said than done when the entire world was against, rather than for, the idea that I should have a family.

Why is it that disabled women and non-disabled women face such contrasting views? No doubt the equating of disability and inability plays a substantial role. We simply do not see disabled women as capable, and mothers are supposed to be endlessly capable, endlessly able. There is no space in the collective imagination for the thought that doing things differently is not the same as doing them badly, nor for the idea that parenting can take many different forms. Despite decades of feminist pressure, our understanding of the role of mothers is still bound up in the physical care-taking of small children, and we think we know how that is done well and how it is done badly. We do not consider that motherhood can look like a million different things, or that being a mother is an emotional, rather than a physical act.

Then, too, there is the constant infantilisation that disabled women face. If we are seen as children, we cannot possibly have children ourselves; the thought is uncomfortable to the point of being disturbing. Infantilisation's fun cousin, desexualisation, is also clearly at play: it is assumed that motherhood must be preceded by (narrowly defined) sex, and so a sexless person cannot be a mother (a notion that is hurtful and offensive to disabled women, those in same-sex relationships and anyone who has had IVF). Perhaps it comes back, once again, to who is seen as a woman at all. Disabled women's supposedly sexless, childlike bodies put us just outside that category of actual womanhood, and so outside the bounds for qualification to be seen as mothers. Whilst it is of course ludicrous to equate womanhood with a desire or a capacity for motherhood, it is undeniable that the two are indelibly linked in the public consciousness. If you are not seen as a real woman, then, you simply cannot be seen as a mother, whether now or in your imagined future. This lack of ability to conceive of disabled women as women at all perhaps explains – but does not excuse – how often disabled women are taken to be the aunts and sisters of their own kids.

This is not to say that disabled men do not face ableism if they become fathers. Dads, after all, are supposed to be fun (let's not even consider the issues here), and disability is seen as distinctly un-fun. Disabled men are also faced with the assumption that disability means inability, and that they will not be able to look after their children. So, yes, disabled men are judged for their decision to have kids. But talking to friends of mine who are disabled men, I am struck by how much less pressure they feel to rectify these issues before these kids actually exist. It's possible that this is simply because thinking about parenthood isn't forced down their throats in the same way it's imposed on women. But I also think it has a lot to do with that pesky perfect-motherhood myth, which expects mums, much more than dads, to meet every single physical and emotional need of their child without any help at all. Disabled women can't do that (because no one can do that!), yet we worry so much about falling short because those expectations are so much higher for us. There seems to be far further to fall.

I internalised this specific brand of sexist ableism to a greater extent than any other. I worried about whether my child would feel unloved because I couldn't get him dressed on the first day of school. I worried about whether my child would be ashamed when her friends saw me in the playground. At the bleakest 4 a.m. moments, I worried about whether, because of all the help I would need from PAs and nannies, my child would even know that I was his mother. Would she rather turn to someone else for love? Would he wish he had different parents? These questions dogged me when friends talked about having kids or even when random adorable children smiled at me from their buggies, pleased as punch to see an adult at eye level. I felt a sickening, pre-emptive guilt about a possible future choice to impose my disability on a child. Was it completely unfair? Was I a bad person for even considering it?

Why exactly I bought so hard into this clearly ableist notion, when I have rejected so many others out of hand, is hard to say. Perhaps it was because, at nineteen, or twenty-three, there was no way for me to prove it wrong. I couldn't exactly borrow a baby and prove that I could mother it. And, of course, because it seemed true: all those bad representations of disabled motherhood were the only ones I had to go off. And also, deep down, even though I was loath to admit it to myself, it was because I cared more about this than I did anything else. I would have given almost anything for the guarantee that I would be a good mum.

Then, slowly, I realised that all of this was – excuse my French – absolute crap. What changed? Well, lots of things. Firstly, while traditional media had absolutely failed to provide any positive representation of disabled parenthood, it turned out that, once again, disabled parents were out there representing themselves. The more I looked, the clearer it became to me that there were disabled parents all over the place, living happy lives with happy children who were, frankly, having a great time. Just type in #disabledparent or #disabledmum to Instagram and watch your feed fill with kids at the park, on playdates, doing crafts and dressing up and having dinner and dancing in the kitchen and going to school and reading stories and singing songs and and and. . . A special shoutout here to my friend Rebekah and her little boy Otto, who are bossing it. As she told me one day, over Zoom, all parents need help; it's just that the help disabled parents need is stigmatised in a way that others' needs aren't. She loves that her son gets to see the value of community; to be truly raised by the village that she has made through the bonds of love and solidarity. What an incredible thing, which made me reconsider my own future need for help raising a child. Rather than seeing a deficit in the things I will not be able to do for them, I now see value: how many more people's love will they feel?

Another of Rebekah's gems of wisdom has also reframed my belief in my ability to be a good parent. She and Otto, she says, are constantly adapting to each other, as all parents and kids do. The evident truth of this statement made me look back at all those times I was sad that I couldn't do something with Stan and Betsy, and reconsider them in a positive light. The truth is that we did always find a way to do what we wanted together, whether by adapting the activity itself or asking for a hand. I like to believe that we learned from each other, whether that was flexibility or the value of collaboration. I can still remember feeling so hurt and guilty when Betsy, perhaps around eighteen months old, put her arms up to me, asking to be picked up, and I couldn't lift her. For years, that moment haunted me. But now I look back and remember what happened next: she simply reassessed the situation and climbed up onto the sofa beside me. In less than a minute, she had what she wanted, which was to be snuggled in my lap. It didn't matter one iota how she got there. I kissed her on the forehead.

This was a pattern repeated throughout the kids' childhoods. There was always a way. We had lots of fun and shared many ordinary, special moments together. A favourite memory from my beleaguered teenage years is going with Lou to pick up Stan, then four or five, from school. She hadn't told him that I would be there, and when he saw me waiting in the playground, his little face lit up and he raced over for a cuddle. He didn't care that I was there in my wheelchair. He didn't even care that other people were staring. He was just happy to see me. To love a child and be loved by them is to know a whole new kind of acceptance.

In a way, then, hanging out with actual kids has dispelled a lot of the hypothetical worries I had. Kids, it turns out, are much less bothered by difference than adults – the real question, for them, is whether you'll let them have pudding for dinner (yes). They're far more willing to adapt in the name of fun and cuddles than adults are in the name of equality and inclusion. The fact is that a lot of the important stuff – bedtime stories and answering the question 'why?' seventeen times in a row – requires no physical ability at all. For a kid, having a disabled adult in their lives is no bad thing, and may actually be good – much fun can be had with a manual wheelchair, a ramp and holding on tight. Thanks, kids, for that invaluable lesson.

Still, I worried that there was a difference between being the fun disabled auntie and a disabled mum. You can't, after all, give your own kids pudding for dinner – at least not every day. The kids I knew and loved only had to adapt to me every now and again – and while I had the example of Rebekah and Otto adapting to each other, I was also acutely aware that she could do a lot more than I will ever be able to. I worried that my disability would just be too much for a child.

These insecurities still plague me. But I found some kind of answer in a conversation I had with my therapist. Endlessly wise and thoroughly no-nonsense, she put it to me that no adult has ever come to her traumatised because their mum wasn't the one to make dinner when they were little. Kids, she told me, need two things: to be cared about, and to know they are cared about. Everything else is just a matter of practicalities. And, she said, she had no doubt I would care beyond all measures of caring.

The more I thought about it, the more this idea became self-evidently true. My parents had, after all, done more than the average amount of physical caring for me, their very disabled kid, yet when I think back to my childhood, I don't remember Dad taking me to the loo or Mum getting me dressed for school. I remember them being at my Christmas plays and telling me stories (Dad's always had a historical setting, Mum's involved animals with funny names). I remember their help in learning my times tables and, later, all the dates for my A-level history exams. I remember birthdays and Christmases and summers playing in the garden. I remember being listened to and made to giggle until my sides hurt. I remember so many things, and precisely none of them involve someone putting my shoes on for me. They all involve being cared about, and knowing I was cared about. Which is to say, they all involve things I could absolutely do with my own kids. I have excellent examples to follow.

In fact, in the past few years, I have performed a slow-but-steady U-turn on the idea I once had of disabled parenting. I now believe, as earnestly as I once believed the opposite, that disabled people make fantastic parents. Maybe that's because I have seen it with my own two eyes, but it's also because I recognise that disabled people have so many of the skills required to be good parents. Adaptability? Check. Military-grade planning? Check. Empathy? Check, check. An understanding that things will go wrong and then be fine? You bet. A friend of mine who has been a nanny for newborn babies remarked to me that most new parents haven't bargained for the complete loss of spontaneity that comes with having a baby. I laughed. I have never been able to be spontaneous in my life. If anyone is prepared for navigating life with a pram, it is me. Perhaps, then, disabled parents aren't good parents despite their disabilities, but because of them. How's that as a retort to meddling comment-makers in the playground?

I realised, too, that if I thought this about other disabled people, I really ought to think it about myself. I thought about it over and over, testing the idea from every angle I could think of, conjuring up imaginary scenarios to see if I could deal with them. And so it was that after over a decade of worry, and at a pace so slow it made me ache, I reached a new conclusion. I would make a good mum. If only I could get there.

For, you see, having (mostly) banished my own internalised ableism, I found there was still plenty of ableism to contend with everywhere else, especially when it came to the matter of actually having a child. I had always assumed I would adopt. It never occurred to me to care about whether a child was biologically mine; it seemed to me that all children need a home and some love, and I could provide those things. Still, my previous fiasco with the dating agency had me worried about other people's ableism stopping me from doing the thing I most wanted in the world. A little voice niggled away in my mind: what if I was turned down for adoption because they, like the dating agency before them, just saw me as too disabled?

My friends seemed to think this was highly improbable, but then again, they'd also been absolutely convinced that the dating agency was the answer to all my problems. I, on the other hand, had long since learned that there were no limits to the depths ableism could plumb, and was thus not so sure. I angsted about it for a while, as I am wont to do, and then I realised that I would never know if I didn't ask. *Put yourself out of your misery*, I thought, *what's the worst they can say to you*?

Well, it turns out the worst they can say to you is exactly what they did say to me. Which was that of course disabled people could adopt, but actually, when it boiled down to it, my own care needs meant I would almost inevitably not be deemed suitable to look after a child in care. Or, to put in another way, disabled people can adopt, but not people as disabled as me. Right.

Is it possible to be completely shocked by something you are expecting? I must have been because I think I actually thanked the woman on the phone before I hung up. It wasn't so much what she'd said, as the way she had said it, as if I was a bit stupid for even asking the question, as if I must not really care about children in care if I thought I would provide a good home in these conditions. I sat and stared at the window, not even looking through it, and then I called my mum and cried.

Once she'd got over her initial concern that I wanted to adopt right now (I did rather spring it on her), Mum very reasonably suggested that the first person I found on a Google search might not be the best person to answer this sort of question. I conceded that she had a point, so I went back to Google and found a much bigger, more established agency to speak to. I took a deep breath and dialled. Surely, I reasoned, I had just been unlucky.

I had not. Granted, the second lady I spoke to was much nicer about it than the first, but she too thought my care needs would be prohibitive to parenting an adopted child. She said that children who have been in care need absolute stability, and, because I could not guarantee that I would have the same PA team for years on end, my home would be deemed unstable. She was sorry, but their absolute duty was to the interests of the child.

The days after these phone calls were perhaps the lowest of my adult life. I couldn't see a way forward. There was – is – no earthly way to make care more stable or reduce my reliance on it. My care situation is one of life's immutable facts, as unchanging as the sequence of the seasons. What was I supposed to do? I struggled to get out of bed. Work passed in a daze. I wondered if the ableism I'd been fighting all my life had, finally, won. I felt physically ill.

Let's just be clear here, this was ableism pure and simple. Everything those two women had said to me (and it became clear, everything other adoption agencies had said to countless other disabled people across the country) was steeped in assumptions about disabled parents that I knew weren't true. Of course, kids who've been in care need ultimate stability, but I wasn't going anywhere. My care needs were only a source of instability if you believed, deep down, that my PAs would be the kid's real parent, because I couldn't possibly be. There was also a pretty whopping double standard. Were they seriously telling me that non-disabled adoptive parents never have help from a nanny, a childminder or a nursery teacher? If handing a child over to a relative stranger for a significant part of the day was totally fine, then why was having some help whilst actively parenting the very worst thing you could do?

To make matters worse, I found the responses to this development from some of those around me to be, well, a little bit ableist. Friends who would never dream of telling me that I shouldn't date or pitch an idea or live independently seemed

oddly keen to tell me how hard it would be to have an adopted
– or indeed any – kid, suggesting that maybe this ableism from
the adoption sector was actually a good thing. I am sure,
knowing them as I do, that in some way, they were trying to
make me feel better, in the same way that you tell people
who've been turned down by their crush that they've dodged
a bullet, but it felt extremely invalidating and, at points, as if
they agreed with the idea that I would be an unsuitable parent.

Then there were the people who disagreed vehemently
with this premise, but seemed to think I could – and should –
challenge the entire system in court. For a while, even I got
swept up in the idea – how good would it feel to take the
Home Office to judicial review and win? – not least because it
gave me a reason to get out of bed. But the more I thought
about it, the more untenable it seemed, especially from an
emotional standpoint. There are only so many battles you can
fight, and I'd waged my fair share, but even more than that, I
couldn't stand the thought of having to prove to an old, white,
posh, almost-certainly-male judge that I could look after a
child. That wasn't what I wanted for myself. It also wasn't the
story I wanted to tell my kids when they asked how we became
a family.

And so it was with a strange sort of grief that I closed the
door on adoption and the life I had imagined for myself. For a
few days I continued to struggle to get out of bed – a feeling I
remembered from my school years – weighed down with the
numb emptiness I felt. Then, I don't know. There was still work
to do. Mum and Dad, the only people in my life who really
know the entirety of what has gone before and what might be
possible, seemed adamant that there were ways around the
problem. And, still, I was only twenty-six. There was time. I
attempted to put the whole thing in a box, if only because I
was scared of the level of despair I felt when I thought about

it. It was easier to pretend that I'd never even called and asked the question; that I'd never heard the answer.

Except, of course, one doesn't forget. Sentences from those two phone conversations would float into my mind, unbidden, haunting. The grief wouldn't lift. My heart ached when I spent time with my baby cousin, or a friend posted a video of a little one learning to crawl. I feared birthdays and the rapid approach of turning thirty. All that time I thought I had started to speed up and collapse in on itself, a process placed on fast-forward when, suddenly, several friends started talking seriously about having kids in the next few years. It was here – the moment I didn't know how to deal with and didn't want to face. I wanted to ignore it all, to push this problem further and further into an imagined future so that it always remained tomorrow's heartbreak, but tomorrow becomes today so quickly.

And then, three weeks before my twenty-eighth birthday, I sat down to write this chapter and realised that I didn't know anything. I had never looked at options other than adopting, and no one had ever mentioned them. I had looked at disabled parenting forums, but I had never posted in them. I had certainly never asked for help. If I was going to write this chapter, I was going to have to take a big, deep breath and finally find out what I needed to know.

The problem is that, even once you have decided to ask for help, there is no obvious person to ask for help from. You are left with the horror of googling your most carefully guarded thoughts, your most deeply held fears, to see if they are true. No one should ever have to do this, and yet there I was trying to come up with different combinations of the phrases 'cerebral palsy', 'wheelchair user', 'single' and 'have a baby'. It would have been funny if it hadn't been so uniquely horrifying. The results separated into two equally unhelpful categories: the ever-familiar advice to parents of disabled kids, and, hallelujah, some advice for women with CP looking to start families. Except. Absolutely every page made reference to abilities I did not have. Almost every page talked about the mother's walking. I do not walk. The information felt as useless as it would have if it hadn't mentioned disability at all. This only reinforced my sense that pregnancy was not for me.

Since the adoption agency slap-in-the-face, I'd been thinking about surrogacy as a possible solution. The child would be biologically 'mine', and under the law, it is rightly much harder for the state to take away your own child than it is to deny you the right to adopt. So, maybe, maybe. A glimmer of hope. But the adoption agency phone calls had made me fear concrete answers, and I hadn't looked into it properly. I was scared. But suddenly, I needed to know. I started reading everything I could find, even though – again – almost none of it was directly relevant to me. There was no mention of disability. I didn't know if this was a good or bad thing, but it felt bad; as if no one like me had ever asked the questions I was asking, let alone succeeded in having a baby this way. But I carried on reading. And then, inevitably, I found the problem: in the UK, a baby born through surrogacy is the legal child of the surrogate until a judge makes a legal order transferring parental rights to the intended parent. The judge can refuse the request if he or she (it's almost always 'he') does not believe that the intended parent would be a better parent than the surrogate. In other words, given everything we know about attitudes to disabled parents, it seemed entirely possible that I could witness the birth of my own child and then have them taken away from me. Just because I am disabled – or, rather, just because of ableism.

At this point, I felt as if I was drowning; a lack of options closing in like water over my head. The familiar despair rose in my chest. I was dizzy; spinning. I needed help. I called home, again, my poor mother once again bombarded with disjointed information, fears and tears. Perhaps this time she was a little less surprised (she knew what I was writing about). I don't remember much of the conversation – I think I was too upset – except for Mum and Dad (who was in the background, trying to help, despite only hearing half of the conversation, poor guy), asking why exactly I'd decided I couldn't have my own kids. I scoffed. 'Because... my body,' I wanted to say, as if that was an entire answer in itself.

Except, over the next few days, I found that I was asking myself the same question. For as long as I could remember, I had fully, wholeheartedly, absolutely, 100 per cent, without-a-shadow-of-a-doubt believed that I couldn't carry a baby. I had told people this fact as if it was immutable. As if I knew it for sure. But, when I really asked myself, when I was honest with myself, I didn't know it for sure. In fact, I had absolutely no idea. I had never asked the question, and no one had ever told me. It was time to put fear aside and face the music.

Vague, stressful googling wasn't really going to cut it. I needed actual specific answers from an actual live human. The question was who; I hadn't seen a doctor for anything directly related to my cerebral palsy for decades. The only person who could possibly help, who knew my body at all, was my physio. If anyone would know, I supposed, it was her. So, desperately trying not to think about how bizarre it was to have this conversation with someone I had known since I was thirteen, I made an appointment for the following week, and waited.

To say I was anxious wouldn't really cover what it felt like for ten years of worry to culminate in a single conversation, but I guess that's just how things go in this weird disabled female life I'm leading. I tried to sound breezy when the physio arrived; tried to act as if this question had just occurred to me, but as I formulated the words, I couldn't look at her. I stared at the Christmas lights I had strung up in the window just that week and tried not to notice that I could hear my own heartbeat. It was one of those moments that you know you'll remember for the rest of your days.

There was absolutely no doubt – not one jot – in my mind about the answer, which I thought would be: 'It wouldn't kill you, but it would be extremely dangerous to you and the baby and you should not under any circumstances do this.' So convinced was I that this would be the response that not only had I (vaguely) mentally prepared myself for it, I had rehearsed what I would say so that I wouldn't sound like I'd just had my heart ripped out. I was ready, come what may. Except I hadn't remotely prepared for what my physio actually did say, which was that she could see absolutely no reason why it would be a problem for me to have my own child.

Wait. What? I looked away from the window to check that I had understood correctly. I blinked, confused, my brain working furiously to process this monumental new piece of information. And then I started to laugh.

Of course, there were caveats and cautions and things that would have to be put in place. But everything I had thought would be an insurmountable problem – from my wonky spine, to my dodgy hips and my muscle spasms – was entirely manageable. When the physio told me that my almost complete inability to walk was, for once, a good thing – a pregnancy wouldn't put any extra pressure on my hips if I didn't walk around – my initial hesitant, nervous laughter turned into a true giggle. I had spent over a decade thinking it was my inability to walk that had weakened my hips so much I couldn't carry a baby. And here I was, twenty-eight-years-old, being told that the exact opposite was true. My inability to walk was going to help me out.

Why was I laughing? Partly from the sheer irony. I mean, really, who would have thought? Partly because I didn't really know what else to do. And partly from a sheer rush of relief, a sugar-high of anguish flowing out of me, my body relaxing, my mind calming, the future feeling lighter, brighter and happier than I could ever have imagined it to be.

It was also partly because the whole thing was so patently absurd. It should never have come to this; me having an awkward conversation after a decade of, at times, profound emotional anguish. Someone ought to have mentioned it; someone ought to have taken seriously my mentions of one day having kids and talked to me about options. Yes, perhaps I also should have asked, but imagine being nineteen and trying to start that conversation. Instead, I was left to those late-night internet searches, those terrifying fears, those doubts and heartaches and feeling so different from the women around me. It didn't have to be this way. So why was it? Simply because no one ever looked at me and saw someone who might one day be a mother.

I certainly feel angry that ableism robbed me of the conversations I deserved to have. I feel let down that I wasn't taken seriously or given the help I needed. But, mostly, I feel deeply sad that my younger self spent so long being afraid of the future when I could have been hopeful; spent so long wanting time to slow down when I could have enjoyed the ride. Society's refusal to see disabled women as women and therefore potential mothers means that we are being failed over and over again, by sex education teachers and medical professionals and advertisers and magazine writers but also, sometimes, accidentally, by the people who love us.

We have been failed, too, by a feminism so (rightly) concentrated on freeing non-disabled women from the sexist obligation to have kids that it never asked about those who faced opposite but equally pernicious assumptions. There were, of course, howls of outrage when the US overturned fifty years of abortion rights – outrage I felt too. But where is the outrage about the forced sterilisation of intellectually disabled women? Where are the campaigns to make sex and pregnancy education inclusive of disabled women? Where are the protests demanding disabled mothers receive adequate social care or against the extraordinary rates at which disabled parents lose access to their kids? What explains these deafening silences is an acknowledgement that the feminist movement, like the society it claims to oppose, holds deeply ableist views on disabled parents and, especially, disabled motherhood. There is also a sense in which feminism is simply too narrow: because most women are unduly pressured to have children, the mainstream movement is not able to work on behalf of those unduly pressured – or indeed forced – not to have them. But these are two sides of the same coin, both formed at their core from that pernicious and familiar myth of the ideal mother.

If feminism really wants to liberate all women from whatever unfair pressures about motherhood they are facing, it should spend some time reimagining what being a mother actually means. It has had quite a lot of success banishing the 1950s housewife caricature – almost no one is complaining these days about women going to work or kids going to nurseries and childminders. But the stereotype has been replaced by another – one equally as damaging and equally exclusionary towards disabled women – of mothers who 'do it all', often single-handedly. How many Instagram memes praise mums as superheroes, meeting all the emotional, physical and often financial needs of their kids and then turning to a bottle of wine when they go to sleep? Why is this considered a good thing? Why does so much supposedly feminist advice presuppose a 'right way' to be a parent that never, ever accounts for differing bodies or abilities? Again, just as with care, modern feminism's obsessive individualism leaves disabled women out in the cold.

As ever, the disability rights movement and disabled people themselves offer the beginnings of a solution – one that could benefit all women, disabled or not. With so many of our positive experiences – good care, finding belonging, making our voices heard – rooted in community and collectivism, I wonder if we cannot find a way to fold those values into our idea of motherhood. I think of Rebecca and her absolute faith that little Otto benefits from the metaphorical village that helps her raise him. I think too of my own future, where any child I had would be inundated with love from the many, many ex-PAs and friends from all parts of my life who form my chosen family. By themselves, each of them would teach a child something brilliant, from how to play the guitar to artistic expression to the importance of being silly, but together they would impart an invaluable lesson: that it is when we are raised by our communities just as much as by our parents that we can lead the fullest lives.

If we could imagine the role of mother as just one in a cast of people who bring up a child, we could free disabled mothers from the extreme judgement and prejudice they face. We could understand disability not as a deficit, or a disadvantage for the child, but as another experience and perspective that they could learn and benefit from. We could recognise the skills that disabled women bring to motherhood – not what they lack – in the form of flexibility, adaptability, self-knowledge and radical acceptance. We could see that all mothers – all parents – have strengths and weaknesses, and we could use that understanding to transform state support so that, instead of trying to catch disabled mothers out and take their kids into care, it instead simply provides the help they need. All of this would, ultimately, help us see disabled mothers as mothers, stopping all those awful comments from the public and suspicions from professionals. It would help us ensure that disabled women and girls are included in conversations about sex, relationships and having kids. It would, eventually, I hope, prevent disabled women who long to be mothers, like me, from feeling how I felt for so long.

This is just one of the ways in which we could expand and diversify our understanding of motherhood. Another is to really focus on what is truly at the heart of being a mother. I don't for one second believe that the essence of being a good mum is making lunch or doing the school run. It is, surely, much more about being there, providing love and support, guidance and fun – the things we remember from our own mothers, but never seem to talk about in the discussion around disabled people and kids. I know that now. I just wish society did too.

I am not naive. I know there will be hurdles galore to jump across, as indeed there always are. As a single woman and a disabled one at that, my ability to have children lies in the hands of the medical profession just as much as my own body. There are so many things that could go wrong. IVF is a cruel Russian roulette for everyone; factor in ableism and it's a truly terrifying prospect. I recently saw a social media post from a disabled woman who was turned away from a clinic because they didn't believe she would be a good mother. The thought of it makes me nauseous. I try to forget that I know this has happened to someone, someone like me, but I can't. I can't shake the fear that something will come up at the last minute to take this away from me.

But I am holding on to newfound hope. Hope that I will one day have a family is a funny thing to be granted in my late twenties, after so many years spent feeling hopeless about it. Don't get me wrong, I am incredibly grateful to have it now, to have a chance at something I never dared to hope for. What a brilliant thing. But it also feels alien, untrustworthy. I keep turning it over in my mind, looking for the weakness that brings down the pack of cards. It is hard to trust that the body I have spent so long hating or ignoring or having to accommodate could in fact be capable of something amazing. It is hard to trust that medical advice, which has been wrong over and over again, could be right this time. It is hard to trust that, after all these years of slowly losing ability, I have abilities I didn't even know about. It is hard to trust that things will work out.

Even if I do get to bring a baby home, things will be complicated. I feel immense guilt about the fact that my kid won't have a dad because society is too ableist to have granted me the opportunity to be a parent with someone. But that pales in comparison to my guilt about the indisputable fact that my child will face ableism from an extremely young age. What will I say to my four-year-old when someone shouts at us that he shouldn't exist? What will I say to my teenager when they're bullied for coming from a home that looks different? Will I be able to find the right words? I hope that a lifetime of living with and writing about ableism will have equipped me with some sort of answer, but I also know that this worry has perhaps more to do with the last vestiges of my internalised ableism than with reality. These things may never happen. Or I may have a kid who is better at calling out ableism than I am. Either way, we'll be OK. If we work these things out together, I'm as sure as I've ever been of anything that we'll get through it.

I'm sure, too, that these difficult moments will be vastly outweighed by good ones, joyous ones, and ordinary, everyday ones too. We will find our own ways, build our own models, create a relationship as unique as any between mother and child. This will be a house full of love. I don't just hope for that. I know it for sure. And that means that I can allow myself to hope for all the other things, too. I am wary of believing. I am wary of hoping. But, for once, I am choosing to. Because, for now, hope is all I need.

Chapter 8

Towards a future where everyone belongs

Ableism is so deeply embedded, so normalised in society, that its many strangling tendrils have become almost invisible. Even I, a woman who has spent over a decade writing about it, can still be surprised – if never quite shocked – by the depths ableism can reach, even as, at the same time, the public remains broadly ignorant that it exists at all. Hopefully this book has shown just how powerful the force of ableism is and lifted the lid on what it is actually like to live in its grasp. The multifaceted, complicated and often contradictory ways it ostracises and devalues disabled people and lives can be slippery and hard to comprehend, but it's vital that we acknowledge the assumptions it's founded on and the ramifications it has.

Ableism is, of course, a systemic problem, but it affects disabled people in profoundly personal ways, from how we're treated on a night out to the relationships that define our lives. The constant message that we are not welcome can become embedded in our psyches and, even once the work of abolishing our internalised ableism is done, leave us on edge and on guard, braced for the next insult. Many of us have become so used to existing like this that we don't even notice a lot of the background ableism we encounter, but that just makes it harder to understand why we feel so anxious, and harder to do anything about it. So I have tried to really uncover the realities of ableism and put words to what is happening. Naming things is powerful, after all.

As the stories in this book have shown, though, to understand, explain and challenge the ableism I was facing, I had to come to understand that it was always in cahoots or in tension with the sexism that is equally prevalent in society. It became more and more obvious that the things that were really bothering me and affecting my life were not just the consequences of one system of oppressive assumptions, but of two. All the ableism I experienced was mixed with and exacerbated by sexism. The more I interrogated the uncomfortable interactions I was having or the assumptions made about who I was, the harder it was to deny the potent misogyny hiding behind all the ways I was being excluded. Sexism and ableism cannot be thought of separately, only as dual forces that buffet the lives of disabled women like me. Almost all of the events detailed in this book happened because of assumptions about disabled women – who we are, what we are capable of and where we belong. The discrimination and prejudice I and those like me face in all areas of life – from the young boy staring in the street to the doctor who denies us sexual healthcare – is predicated on the idea that we are less capable, less worthy, less human than everyone else. Yes, this is true for all disabled people, but far more so for disabled women, as we face multiple systems of marginalisation. My life is evidence that the consequences of this compounded discrimination are social and political. But they are also personal. After all, the intricate intertwining of ableism and sexism throughout my life has shaped me at every turn and on every level, affecting the way I feel about myself, the choices available to me and, most crucially, how I relate to those around me.

Yet, no matter where or how keenly I looked, I never saw this intersectionality properly acknowledged, let alone openly discussed. And no matter how obvious to me this crucial interplay between ableism and sexism became, it remained equally and painfully obvious that the non-disabled society around me was largely oblivious to it. This made it so much trickier to hold on to what I knew and move forward. I became increasingly frustrated by society's failure to see what was going on, until, slowly, I realised: it was up to me. I was going to have to teach everyone else what I'd come to understand. And thus I started writing this book.

I never intended to write a memoir. Indeed, for many years I went around insisting that I wouldn't. I'd tell someone one of the many stories you have just read, and they'd say, 'You should really write a book.' And I would laugh and demur and say 'No, no, I couldn't possibly.'

There was the obvious issue, which is that books are long and my party trick has always been coming in well under word count. The idea that I would somehow spin out tens of thousands of words – enough for *a book* – seemed laughable. But that wasn't the main source of my reluctance to countenance sitting down to write this story. The truth is, I didn't want to write about disability. I know, I know, I have done quite the U-turn.

The story of how I got to be here, writing this book, is not exactly linear. I decided that journalism was for me around the age of twelve, when I realised I loved writing but had absolutely no ability – none whatsoever – to create a plot. In journalism, I reasoned, the plot was there for you. Ideal. I set up a blog and started writing. And it turned out I was fairly good at it. So I kept going.

Let's not forget that during my teenage years I was trying extremely hard to be as least disabled as possible. Naturally, then, it didn't occur to me to write about disability. I resolutely ignored all the advice to 'write what you know' and instead wrote about the news I saw on the telly. Looking back, it is hard to know whether to be embarrassed or impressed with my fifteen-year-old self's willingness to write about the Arab Spring and the US Tea Party movement. But at least I was writing. The blog became my solace, something good to focus on while everything else spiralled.

When I started going on work-experience placements in my late teens, things became a little more complicated. For one, a lot of local papers and small magazines have offices that aren't accessible. More confusingly, I got a lot of contradictory advice. Editors would encourage me not to be pigeonholed; to write about the things other than disability that interested me. But as a nineteen-year-old just starting out in freelance journalism, pieces on disability were the only ones I could reliably get commissioned. And once published, my disability pieces were the only ones to receive attention. Some of the very same editors who warned against pigeonholing also advised me to use the media's desperation for diverse voices to get my foot in the door.

Personally, I didn't want everything I did to be about disability. So much of my non-working life was about access and care and ableism. I didn't want writing – one of the few things I could do completely independently – to be dominated by the same subjects. I thought my life should be, *ought* to be, about more than disability. And I thought my other interests were somehow more legitimate and intellectual. Writing about disability, then, became a means to an end. I still believed that this work wasn't a real job – or, at least, that I would do it until I got a real job reporting on foreign affairs or politics or some such thing. And the thing is, it kind of worked. By the time I was twenty-two, I had parlayed my freelance disability writing into a proper, grown-up job in the BBC's main newsroom, and a year later I was reporting from Westminster. I loved what I was doing. It was great fun. And having spent my teenage years worrying that my disability and ableism would stop me from getting a job, and working furiously hard in order to prove myself, I felt like I'd finally made it. Maybe I could relax.

Except, I wasn't very happy. Because for the first time ever, I couldn't write about disability even when I wanted to. The BBC's strict impartiality rules made it almost impossible to report disability stories when I felt so strongly that there was a clear right and wrong. And, in all honesty, because the BBC still primarily sees disability as a medical issue – not the social and political one I know it to be. It all felt pretty limiting and infuriatingly contradictory, because the BBC kept claiming it was trying to better represent the diverse communities it is supposed to serve.

There were so many ways that the media was failing disabled people. Every day, it seemed, I stumbled across a story peddling a disabled person's trauma, or using a disabled kid's achievements to help non-disabled people feel better about their own lives (both equally gross sides of a coin we like to call 'inspiration porn'). Tabloids screamed headlines about disability benefit 'fraudsters', while broadcasters ran pieces equating being disabled with poor quality of life. Inequalities and struggles were portrayed as natural consequences of disability rather than as a result of rampant discrimination. No one ever – ever – mentioned ableism.

As my fury grew, so did an uncomfortable sense of guilt. Cocooned (read: trapped) in the rarefied environment of a global broadcaster, I wondered if my enforced silence made me in some way complicit. I had the skills and platform to make some noise about the ableism I could see all around me, but I wasn't. Was I letting the side down? All around me, as I became more embedded in my community, I could see other disabled people doing the work. And as I watched them, I realised that maybe my reluctance to make my life 'about disability' was not a sign of empowerment but the exact opposite. Perhaps, really, it was the last vestiges of my internalised ableism. Why else did I believe that anti-ableism work was somehow less valuable than reporting the same old dross from Parliament? Why did I think that writing about disability meant 'pigeonholing' myself, and why was that necessarily a bad thing? Why was I pretending that this wasn't the thing that got me out of bed in the morning? I looked around and thought: why am I letting ableist attitudes influence my career goals? My guilt mixed with annoyance at myself.

This nagging unease was supercharged by the Covid pandemic and my frankly through-the-looking-glass experience of covering the government's daily press conferences. As I copied down the same banal Matt Hancock platitudes day in, day out, messages kept pouring in about disabled people infected by unmasked social-care staff, about crucial care packages revoked as councils redirected funds, about families of very ill kids unable to get their usual PPE because the government had compulsorily purchased it for the NHS. And the worst ones of all: messages from distraught family members of learning-disabled or elderly people whose GPs had decided to issue them with Do Not Resuscitate orders that would deny them care if they got really sick. I would look back to my live feed of that day's press conference and wonder what the hell I was doing.

I think that, up until Covid, I had naively and perhaps subconsciously believed that, as more and more disabled people became visible and successful, ableism would naturally weaken its grip on society – and on us. But the pandemic showed that any veneer of progress was millimetres thick; when it came down to it, the government and wider society were willing to sacrifice disabled people's health – and lives – for an all-too-soon return to the pub. And on social media, on TV, even in the pages of national newspapers, they didn't even feel the need to pretend otherwise.

Eventually, though, what tipped the scale – what made me take the leap and quit my job – was much more personal. My reckoning with the unfathomable strength of ableism when it came to Covid happened at the exact same time as I was personally left reeling by the two most painful instances of ableism I had experienced since I was a teenager: the rejections from the dating and adoption agencies. A microcosm of what was happening in society was happening in my own life; the illusion of acceptance I'd gained through success in my career had shattered, exposing the many ways I was still viewed as the other, an outsider, not worthy of the happy family life I longed for. I was hurt, but I was also profoundly angry. It had been almost a decade since I'd escaped school, but society was still as prejudiced as the teenage girls who had bullied me. It wasn't getting better; indeed, as I moved into my late twenties, it all seemed to be getting worse again. And, as the questions of dating and motherhood took on a new urgency, I realised that I could no longer afford to just carry on as I was, hoping – in vain – for change. I had to start making it happen. In the end, quitting my once-dream job wasn't even a difficult decision. The dream had changed. Or I had. Either way, I knew with absolute certainty that I had a voice and I wanted to use it. And I also had a vague inkling that an idea for that book I was never going to write was forming in my head – getting louder, stronger, more urgent as the silence around disabled womanhood began to ring angrily in my ears. I decided I had to write it. And to do that, I had to work for myself, so I left the BBC and went freelance.

My job now is more fulfilling than I could possibly have imagined when I was busy trying to avoid disability. I spend my days raising awareness and hopefully changing minds – whether that's by interviewing disabled people about their stories in national newspapers; sharing my own experiences in this book, my newsletter or on social media; or speaking at events and conferences. I can't believe I am lucky enough to make a living by talking to people I admire – disabled people in media, entertainment, politics, business – and sharing what I learn from them with as many people as I possibly can. Being able to do this work, being trusted by members of my community to tell their stories with and for them, is an absolute privilege. It feels urgent and necessary and never, ever, a waste of time. It is hard and infuriating and often feels, when I'm explaining the social model for the five hundred and seventy-third time, like banging your head against a wall; but it is also exhilarating, empowering and deeply meaningful. And, often, a hell of a lot of fun. I am happier than I have ever been.

Whenever I'm writing or speaking, I have a few core aims in mind. First and foremost, I want to demystify and destigmatise disability, especially disabled womanhood. For so many, disability remains something shrouded in secrecy and shame. I try to show what being disabled is really like, and why it is no bad thing. This naturally leads to my next aim: helping people see disability through the social model. Over and over, I emphasise that the problems and inequalities associated with disability are created by society; that they are not inevitable or preordained but a result of persistent, widespread and deeply embedded discrimination. This, in turn, takes me on to goal number three: lifting the lid on the nature of ableism and the multiple, insidious ways it can influence disabled people's lives. I try to challenge the stereotypes and incorrect assumptions that underpin this ableism, and to replace them with a solid base of understanding from which equality and inclusion can be built. Then it's on to finding solutions, whether by interviewing the experts or empowering people to become activists and allies themselves.

Along the way, I make sure that everything I do highlights intersectionality. Disability is an oft-overlooked element of a diverse society, but the diversity within disability itself is ignored even more. Of course, unless I am interviewing, I can only speak for myself, and I hope one day we hear much more from and about the experiences of queer disabled people, disabled people of colour, neurodivergent people, chronically ill people, learning-disabled people and non-verbal people, all of whom I cannot possibly claim to represent. What I can do, though, is shout loudly about my experiences of disabled womanhood and how those two identities interact and combine into something more than the sum of their parts. It is time that we recognised the different experiences disabled women have, and indeed that we are here at all. And it is time we – or I – talked about them.

So that's what this book is for. I hope that in sharing a little of what it's been like to live as a disabled woman for the past twenty-eight years, I have exposed some of the sexism and ableism that are both so widespread and so deeply ingrained in society. But I also hope I have shown that these forces do not act separately, but in unison, combining as often as they contradict, creating situations not just of being a woman or of being disabled, but specific and particular to being a disabled woman. The stories in this book reflect what it is like to navigate life from this distinct position – and how the intertwining of disability and womanhood, sexism and ableism, makes our experience of each unique.

Indeed, the common thread that best links the struggles I had as a teenager with body image and friendships to the complicated realities of dating and motherhood that have dominated my twenties is the exclusion of disabled women from the social understanding of womanhood itself. It can be seen in everything from the seemingly innocuous inaccessibility of women's fashion to the horrifying effects of desexualisation, from the perniciousness of bullying to the cultural silence around disabled motherhood. In each case, disabled women are excluded from spaces of feminine identity, whether that be a tight-knit friendship circle or a nail salon, and this has real effects on where we are deemed to, and deemed not to, belong. There continues to be a denial of the basic fact that disability and womanhood can and do co-exist.

But disabled women *do* exist. We are here. And we need to be recognised in our own right because the experiences I have shared here go to show that our experiences of disability differ from those of disabled men, while our experiences of womanhood are often the exact inverse of those of our non-disabled counterparts. The problems we face, from desexualisation to decisions on motherhood, body image to our place in friendship groups, are the opposite of those faced by other women. This means that, although the disability rights movement is far from perfect, it is mainstream feminism that most profoundly fails to include disabled women and contributes to our ostracism and invisibility.

So while this book is about many things, it is actually mostly about belonging and not belonging. Most fundamentally, I had to find belonging in my own body; to resist persistent and powerful narratives that it was at once separate from me and a source of great shame, a reason for my exclusion. All my life, I have been told by misogynist ableism that the disabled, female body I live in is broken, ugly and a problem to be ignored because it cannot be fixed. Alongside this stigmatisation, disabled women's bodies are physically exiled as a matter of routine, from being denied access to the loo in a restaurant to a dearth of hoists in maternity wards. Totted up across many individual lifetimes, this continual physical exclusion, particularly from traditionally feminine spaces, contributes significantly to our conceptual exclusion from the very category of women and the social belonging that it can confer.

From there, so many other forms of women's or feminine belonging become, if not impossible, at least hard to navigate.

Friendships become fraught, because we are told that female friendships are based on shared experiences. When the experiences of womanhood are denied to one member of the group, all of its participants wonder if there is enough commonality, and all worry about whether they can relate to each other's lives deeply enough to maintain strong bonds. For disabled teenage girls, especially, exclusion from the trappings of girlhood can lead to profound social isolation, ostracism and bullying – all with lifelong effects on a person's self-confidence and worth. Even for adult disabled women, the difficulty of not sharing, of not moving through life at the same speed or in the same way as the non-disabled women we know and love, can be extremely painful, another part of life in which we can feel we do not belong.

This is why community is so important. Yet even there, young disabled women are often denied access to their community because ableism and sexism make it so hard to find. Disabled people are kept out of the media, entertainment and politics – and this is only more true for disabled women – meaning that lots of us grow up feeling completely alone, as if no one else shares our experiences. There appears to be no one who can understand and, perhaps most painfully, no role models providing an example to follow. So many of us have been left floundering by the cultural silence around disability and disabled womanhood. This is incredibly damaging to our mental health, and creates a sense of isolation and being the odd-one-out that can persist long after we have found and built our own communities.

Even once those communities have been forged, it's important to acknowledge that silences remain. While I am lucky to now spend life surrounded by brilliant disabled women, our particular experiences are some of the least acknowledged in the disability rights movement because so often it is disabled men who are given the mic, and therefore the effects of sexism on ableism are easily ignored. If disabled women are to feel that we really belong, the issues highlighted in this book must be given more prominence within our own community.

This is especially true of the particular circumstances disabled women face in the world of dating. At every turn, disabled women are met with a toxic mix of desexualisation, infantilisation and open-mouthed curiosity that makes dating an absolute nightmare for many of us. Once again, the consequences of society's failure to see disabled women as women leave us distressingly marginalised. The constant rejection and dehumanisation are hard enough to deal with in and of themselves, but perhaps the most difficult thing about disabled women's exclusion from dating and relationships is the related exclusion from so many cultural touchstones and personal milestones, and the many ways this stops us from belonging in society in general.

The most painful ramification of the denial of disabled women's womanhood is, at least for me personally, our exclusion from the cultural, medical and personal conversation around motherhood. In society's eyes, womanhood and motherhood are indelibly linked – if you're seen as not fully belonging to the former category, you cannot possibly hope to enter the latter. This leads to all kinds of horrible things, from disabled women being denied sexual healthcare to kids being taken away from their parents just because those parents are disabled. Even at the marginally less horrific end of the scale, the cultural silence around disabled motherhood can leave disabled women like me feeling as if we cannot start families or that, if we do, we'll be terrible mothers to even the most longed-for children. We are made to feel that, in regards to motherhood, we should not even try to belong.

At every turn, then, disabled women are denied the chance

to fully belong in the spaces, structures and ideas of womanhood. But that's not the end of the story. Because, as often as disabled women are excluded, we are remaking and rewriting the very terms of that belonging, and the very definition of womanhood. This has been the essential work of this book and of my life, and will continue, I am sure, to be the core of my disability activism for many years to come.

Every single lesson in this book I learned the hard way, by slowly unravelling everything ableism and sexism had led me to believe was true about where and how I belonged. The first, difficult lesson was in unpicking the ways ableism and sexism had divorced me from my own body. The social model of disability was instrumental in helping me to stop blaming my body for the exclusion I faced, and understanding that the blame lay instead with an ableist and sexist society. This allowed me to stop disliking my physical appearance by redefining body positivity as a radical body acceptance, and to recognise that it was the world that was not built for me rather than that I wasn't built for the world. The certainty of this knowledge has waxed and waned over the years, but learning it again and again has always been a good thing. Eventually, the social model allowed me to bridge the divide society had forced me to build between myself and my body, and I was able to find belonging in my own physicality – even liking what I see in the mirror. Finally, I was able to claim womanhood itself for this disabled, female body, and thus find some belonging in the idea of femininity I had long felt excluded from.

I also had to unlearn everything sexism and ableism had taught me about independence and reliance, and what my relationship to these ideas meant for my place in the world. In a society that valued doing things for yourself and saw asking for help as the ultimate sign of weakness, it took some rewiring to see the beauty in interdependence, the strength in relying on support. But the beauty and strength *is* there, and they provide the foundation for some of the deepest relationships I have been lucky enough to experience. The bonds I share with my girls – PAs past and present – are incredibly powerful, based on a radical and complete acceptance of each other's needs and creating a camaraderie that I have never seen replicated elsewhere. We truly are in it together; there is no sense of belonging like it.

Most rewarding, perhaps, has been redefining what good female friendships (outside caring) look like, and what we can mean to the people we love. Once I realised that the expectation to share all our life experiences was a product of sexist, ableist homogenisation, it became much easier to see how much we gain when we celebrate our differences. I have learned so much from witnessing and respecting the diversity of my friends' experiences – whether related to disability or not – and my own life is richer, brighter and frankly much more fun for it. It can be hard, of course, when the people whose thoughts I most value cannot understand a particular disability-related problem, but I also recognise that it is in trying to understand, in the listening anyway, and in a quiet but complete acceptance that they show their care. Belonging, then, is not the 'fitting in' I once believed it to be, but an act of being met with love exactly where you are.

The best lesson yet has been learning and defining the power of community. I have discovered that you don't really have to know someone to be indelibly bonded to them by ties of support and solidarity. There is immense power in recognising yourself in a tweet, or in a smirk fired across a room. The disability community has not only taught me about the giddy joy that comes from feeling completely at ease in a room full of strangers, but also, thanks to gifting me some disability pride, what it is to feel completely at ease with yourself, and the profound sense of belonging that comes with both.

Some lessons remain a work in progress, but the process of redefining belonging is in full flow. My feelings around dating, as is clear from this book, remain complicated. On this particular issue, I have decided for the sake of my mental health not to attempt to single-handedly dismantle the mile-high wall of sexist ableism I face, but, instead, to redefine what it means to live a happy life, full of different kinds of love. I still feel excluded, but perhaps not so much as I used to, and at least I am not being painfully confronted by that exclusion as often as I once was.

The last lesson in this book was undoubtedly the hardest to learn. I have had to redefine what it might mean to belong in my own future family and in the role of a mother. While I am not actually there yet, I have done a lot of the conceptual work already – not least through writing this book! I have dismantled the sexist ableism that says motherhood is a certain thing and that disabled women cannot possibly embody it, and now I frankly do not believe either of these things to be true. Motherhood is simply an act of love, and everyone can do that. There is something radically empowering about redefining parenting – the hows and whys and with whos – to something that is much more expansive and inclusive, and to which so many more people can belong. Including me.

I had to learn these lessons pretty much by myself; there isn't exactly a map to follow or advice in the pages of *Cosmo*. At times it has felt like a slog, but actually there has been a lot of joy, laughter and fun along the way. I have made peace with my body and its need for care, learned a lot about myself through dating and considering motherhood and, most happily, surrounded myself with friends and a community I adore beyond all measure. In amongst it all, I have found that the world and its assumptions about womanhood were wrong.

There is room for us all to belong in the sisterhood. We simply need to broaden and expand our definitions, remake our understandings and claim our place.

These new definitions of belonging are precious to me, but they shouldn't have been so hard to come by, and living by them shouldn't put me at odds with almost everyone else. So it cannot just be down to people like me to spread them and use them to forge a more inclusive society. In order to lift the lid on the intersection of disability and womanhood and show what it is like to live at it, this book has told a very personal story. My story. But now it is over to you.

Disabled people – disabled women – need allies. We need non-disabled people to stand up against the ableism and sexism that can make life so difficult. We need non-disabled people to speak up when things are wrong or unfair or exclusionary. And we need non-disabled people to join us in the fight to make them better.

The first step, obviously, is having a good sense of what the problems are. For that, you need to listen to disabled people, particularly disabled women, online and in your own life, or read what we have to say (this book is a good start but not enough!). Seek out our voices. We're here to be heard.

But there are also tangible, practical ways to help. The most obvious thing to do is to challenge inaccessibility – whether you are with a disabled person or not. Ask shops, restaurants and pubs why they don't have ramps or braille signage or hearing loops and – here's the crucial part – say that you won't be coming back until they get them. It's particularly important to do this in the spaces where disabled women are most excluded – an emphasis on the need for disabled loos certainly wouldn't go amiss. If you can, be explicit about it – say that you don't want to give your hard-earned cash to businesses that discriminate. Money speaks louder than words. Spurring public spaces to become more accessible is one of the easiest and most effective ways to make society more inclusive.

Take your allyship to work, too. Ask about flexible working policies and whether recruitment processes bar good candidates with different experiences. Offer to do the research on how to make your workplace more inclusive or, better yet, encourage your bosses to hire an actually disabled access consultant. Outside work, too, you can do all sorts of things, like making sure the disabled kid in your child's class is not only invited to but included in parties, or voting for governments that prioritise social care. You can complain when the media casts disabled people as lazy stereotypes. And you can buy Christmas presents from disabled-led or -owned small businesses. These might seem like small, inconsequential actions, especially set against the vast mass of ableism, but every change is a disabled person's life improved in some way, and that adds up to more than you could possibly imagine.

Still, as this book has shown, these little tangible things won't be enough. We need to challenge the damaging assumptions made about disabled people and disabled women. We need to understand how ableism operates and how it interacts with sexism, and then we need to work to rid society of both. And fundamentally, we need to change, expand and develop our understanding of womanhood to include disabled women.

This book has shown some of the ways you can do that. The first and most profound shift you can make is to see the world through the clarifying lens of the social model. Once you no longer see disabled people's bodies and minds as the essential problem, it is much easier to avoid making ableist assumptions about them. This singular change can lead to many more. We can stop seeing disabled bodies as less than or broken. We can stop pitying the people who live in these bodies. We can make space and accommodate bodies in all their diversity, whether that's through physical accessibility or valuing rest or making a wider range of clothes. For disabled women, in particular, one of the most important things the social model can help us with developing is a better, more inclusive understanding of body positivity, one that is not predicated on looks or ability but on every body's inherent value. When we stop labelling some bodies as bad and some as good, we free ourselves from many of the ableist and sexist judgements disabled women – and, really, everyone – are so often subjected to. This might all seem theoretical or abstract, but creating a world underpinned by the social model is within your power. You can choose carefully how you speak about bodies and minds – yours or anyone else's – whether that's not equating ability to worth or not equating difference with unattractiveness. And you can work to remove the physical and attitudinal barriers that disable those of us who are excluded by the ableist and sexist society we live in.

We also need to radically rethink our ideas about care, the people providing that care, and the people receiving it. The social model encourages us to see people's needs as neutral, rather than a sign of weakness or a cause for pity. From there, we can see that care is just a meeting of those needs, and that care is fundamentally enabling. If we strip away ableist and sexist notions about the value of independence, we can replace them with an inclusive understanding of the power and worth of interdependence, and from there we can stop seeing people who need care as failures. We can also treat those doing the caring – overwhelmingly women – a whole lot better. Doing so would prevent so many people feeling shame and instead empower them to ask for what they need. I challenge you to resist the societal urge to look away, to cover up the reality of care, and to instead look at care, and really see the people behind it and the opportunities it creates for rich, fulfilling lives and deep, glorious friendships.

We can make other friendships easier to enjoy, too, especially for young disabled girls. We need to model inclusion to our kids, by talking about disability and differences of all kinds, so that when they go to school they are primed to be accepting. One of the most powerful things we can do is be alert to, call out and put a stop to bullying when we see it, saving these girls from a lifetime of rebuilding themselves. As adults, too, we should be much more willing to have friends with vastly different life experiences. We should make the spaces where friendships are forged (after-work drinks, for example) much more accessible, but we should also challenge the ableist and sexist structures that value conformity. We should celebrate our differences, and build friendships on mutual respect for each other. That way, we can move past the rigid understanding of fitting in that leaves disabled women out in the cold and create a world where anyone can belong.

If we really want to help young disabled people, especially girls, we can make sure they have proper access to their community. The first step to doing that is making the disability community much more visible, in newspapers and magazines and books and on the telly. Everywhere. You can make this happen, by supporting and sharing the disabled storytelling you do see. Full, authentic disabled stories should be part of the culture, so that non-disabled people can see the value of our voices. But also so that young disabled people can see themselves represented and not feel so alone, so that they can build their own spaces of community and friendship.

Quite clearly, one of the most important things we can do to improve life for disabled women is to make the dating scene less of a cesspit of sexist ableism. We desperately need a new, more inclusive understanding of attractiveness, and to radically free ourselves from the deeply harmful, old-fashioned gender roles that so limit who is seen as worthy of intimacy and relationships. Schools need to provide all their pupils with relevant sex education, and disabled women of all ages need to be empowered with information and support. As a society, we need to change our language so that we create a new world, where we see that everyone is worthy of love.

Lastly, we need to stop excluding disabled women from the realm of motherhood. We need to remake sexual and maternal services to be accessible and inclusive, and to stop services for parents from actively discriminating against disabled mothers. For this, the healthcare professionals, journalists and activists among you need to step up. But we also need a wholesale reimagining of who we think can or should be mothers, and for that we need to continually dismantle the myth of perfect motherhood. We need to talk about the countless ways there are to be a good mother, and how all of us – disabled or not – rely on a village to raise our kids. Once again, you have the power to help with this, whether by being careful not to use exclusionary language or by simply not awkwardly avoiding a disabled mum at school pick-up time. We can make motherhood for everyone who wants it, if only we try a little harder.

It is time, too, for a new feminism. A feminism that recognises the particular maelstrom of oppression faced by disabled women. A feminism that sees these issues as just as important to dismantle, no matter how much they appear to contradict those faced by non-disabled women. A feminism that understands that there are different bodies and needs and experiences. A feminism that is inclusive. A feminism that insists that non-disabled women are women. A feminism that fights for – and belongs to – everyone.

We all have a responsibility to create a better future. History tells us that it can be done, that change is possible. If we do this right, if we write the world anew so that inclusion and self-acceptance and love in all its forms are easier to find for disabled women, perhaps there'll be a young disabled girl out there who takes a less winding road to belonging.

Acknowledgements

Well. Writing this book has been the culmination of so much good fortune that it is hard to know where to start with thanking the people who created it. But start I must. Here goes.

To Anna Mishcon, my friend and mentor, the first person to help bring this book to life. Thank you for the endless help and advice, and for always championing me.

To Jess Molloy, my fantastic agent at Curtis Brown, who instinctively understood what I was trying to do. Thank you for navigating me through this terrifying, exciting time.

To Marleigh Price and Izzy Holton, my extremely talented editors at DK. Thank you for believing in this book, keeping me calm (ish), and for your endlessly wise thoughts and suggestions – it has been a complete joy to work with you. Thanks also to the rest of the team at DK.

Other people have helped this book come about in less tangible ways. Three women in particular have been there as I've teased out the ideas and situations that make up this memoir.

To Nalina, who has listened to some of my deepest anxieties and never judged. Thank you for your kindness and wisdom.

To Sophie, my oldest friend, who is proof that good things are to be found in hard times and who never fails to make me feel better. Thank you for always being there. I love you lots.

To Rachel, my partner in crime. I would be absolutely lost

without you. Thank you for the many hours spent deconstructing ableism, the many more spent laughing, and for being the person I can say my wackiest thoughts to. You are brilliant. I adore you.

Enormous thanks to my Warwick crew, Becky, Becky, Alex and Josh, for teaching little Luce the meaning of friendship, and being my biggest cheerleaders ever since. You are, simply, the best.

And of course, my boys, without whom I would never have had the confidence to write this book. I cannot possibly say enough, but let me try.

To Alex, thank you for being my safe haven all these years and somehow always turning my tears into laughter. Thanks also for marginally improving my music taste.

To Paul, thank you for the constant reassurance, the unfailing support, and all the times I have laughed so hard I've feared for my own safety. Thanks also for telling me when necessary that I'm being an idiot.

Thanks to you both for the knowledge that I will never be lonely again. I love you.

To my community, raucous, hilarious, full of solidarity and, marvellously, ever expanding. Thank you for all the support, encouragement and fun. Thank you for creating spaces where we all belong. I hope I have done you proud.

To my girls, without whom nothing good in life, including this book, would be possible. Thanks for giving me my freedom and, you know, keeping me alive.

To Laura K, thank you for all your patience at school, and the confidence you had that things would get better. I miss the fun we had.

To my university girls – Fran, Hayley, Em, Gisela and Fran F – thank you for the best three years of my life, happy memories to last a lifetime, and giving me the best possible start to this adulthood lark. I am eternally grateful.

To my South London babes – Rachy, Tilly, Charlie and Ruby – thank you for always, always keeping the show on the road. Thank you for all the late-night chats, all the hugs, and the many, many things you have all taught me along the way. Thank you for filling this little flat with love, laughter, dancing and not an insignifIcant amount of rum. I feel so lucky to be sharing life with you.

To Ania and Laura, my adopted big sisters. Thank you for the ways you have pushed and encouraged me. Thank you for the adventures – in London and beyond – and all the quiet days in the flat. Thank you for sticking by me when the going got tough, and for how safe you made me feel when Covid made it seem like the apocalypse was nigh. Thank you for turning the flat into a comedy stage every single day. Thank you for becoming my family. I love you so much.

And to Georgia, who appeared in my life in this intense year of memoir writing and care upheaval, and faced it all with a big grin and endless enthusiasm. Thank you. I cannot wait to see what mischief we get up to next.

And finally, special thanks to my family, blood and made, for always believing.

To the kids – Stan and Betsy – of whom I am so proud I could burst. Thank you for filling life with joy and being the best thing to ever happen to me. I love you to the moon and back.

To my Lou, who I simply cannot imagine life without. Thank you for the best childhood a person could have, and for always, always answering the phone. Thank you for always encouraging me to try again, to do the scary thing, and for being there when it all gets too much. Thank you for being my real-life fairy godmother. I love you more than all the words in this book could say.

To Mum and Dad, simply the best parents I could ever have wished for. Thank you for the belief that I would find my own way, and the knowledge that you would be there every time I floundered. Thank you for doubting all the naysayers. Thank you for making me laugh even when things are tough, and teaching me to celebrate when they are good. Thank you for answering the phone even when I've already called three times that day, for fixing everything I am always breaking, and coming over just because I want you to. Thank you for teaching me to stand up for myself, and supporting my slightly mad decisions (like quitting my job to write a book) when others would shake their heads. Thank you for ensuring I knew I could go out into the world and change it. Thank you, really, for everything. A million 'I love you's would never be enough.